A SURVIVOR'S STORY OF BEEN IN STATE CARE I WAS BORN MIDLY INTELLECUALLY HANDICAP

ZERO TOLERANCE AGAINST CHILD SEXUAL ABUSE

Suffered Abuse (RAPE) at Stanmore Road Boys Home and Campbell Park School and other family homes. The Department of Social Welfare aka Ministry of Child Youth & Family aka Oranga Tamariki had Duty of Care and they failed Duty of Care. Oranga Taramiki is still failing children now so wake up and stop the abuse and the lieing and cover ups Oranga Tamaiki. **No one from my current life is in this book .**

DEDICATION

This book is dedicated to all the victims of abuse (RAPE) at Campbell Park School, Stanmore Boys Home and foster homes in New Zealand Department of Social Welfare care and Hospitaller Order of Saint John of God (Saint John of God Brothers) care (Roman Catholic Church) .

And to Judy Moore and Fiona Wilson, Garth Young of Care Claims and Resolutions and Sonja Cooper of Cooper Legal , Wellington New Zealand. And Peter Karp of Karp O'Neill Lawyers in Sydney, Australia.

And to Kris Robinson, Nicola Redmond & Karen Smith & Taren Sinclar & Tex Everett & Grant West, Kara Lynn and Michael Dooley Bishop of Dunedin, Darryl Baser & Vic Tamati and Kathy Devine, Dr Murray Peter Heasley and Liz Tonks & Lynette Stevens, Michael Chamberlain, Adam Cassidy & Tony Kokshoorn Mayor of Grey District Council and Dame Susan Devoy, Murray Graves, Alan Graves, Margaret & Keith Fraser, Chris Morris from ODT (Otago Daily Times), MK Albie & MK Rob Epere & Aprill Mokomoko and Mark Grott , Ken Clearwater of Male Survivors Aotearoa and Dugal Armour & Bill Young & Tone Miller of MSSAT Otago/ Southland for their support. James Egan co-President of The Archangle Foundation, Inc of Chicago, Ilinois, USA. Fred Coughlan a close friend & Ingrid Leary & Nigel Latta and Jim Clemente Retired FBI Agent,PACT Apartment Dunedin & Justin Payne Pedrophile Hunter my hero, Piripi Rakete, Ron Marks & Mark Dekkers, Glenys Dickinson, Stephen Lynch & Sarah Elizabeth Murphy, Dan Sherwood, Lenoa Huggins & Marita Murphy, Shaun Dougherty & Phil Savino, Tim Lennon & Jami Lee Ross MP founder of Advance NZ politicial party, Kylie Batten Dunedin Police.

Sue Astle a good and a dear friend who I see has a sister. Corinda Taylor chairperson at Life Matters Suicide Prevention Trust does a lot of work for the community. Jo Turner lawyer/friend at Communtiy Law Otago.

And wish to thank the support of Border Control & Customs of New Zealand for the work they are doing to protect New Zealand from sick sex offenders coming to New Zealand.

Darryl W Smith(c)2020 Published by

 PRESS

First Edition 2020

ACKNOWLEGEMENT

Sonja Cooper of Cooper Law & Chris Morris of Otago Daily Times Ministry of Education and CEO Brendon Boyle of Ministry of Social Development & Collen Boyd poet and friend, Grant Cameroon & Assocations, Legal Aid Services.

Care Claims & Reslution team Garth Young & Judy Moore, Fiona Wilson.

Members of Parliament at the time.

Simon Power, Lianne Dalzeil, Ruth Dyson, Annette King, Jim Anderton, Christopher Hobyson, John Key, Dr Mariel Newman, Craig McNair and Steve Maharey & Georgina Beyer, Trevor Mallard & Pete Hodgson, Peter Dunne, Dr Michael Cullan & George Hawkins, Tim Barnett, John Hayes, Amy Adams & Jo Goodhew, Pansy Wong & Gerry Brownlee and others.

SPECIAL THANKS TO THE NEW ZEALAND POLICE FOR FIGHTING AGAINST CHILD ABUSE.

FORWARD

I am honored to be asked by Darryl to write this forward for his book Silent No More about the abuse (rape) he suffered in State Care. Darryl's second book in the series of his journey.

I first meet Darryl in 2002 when another man I was working with "Patrick" went public about the sexual abused he suffered at the hands of the Brothers at the St John of God school in Halswell, Christchurch. Aka Hospitaller Order of Saint John of God.

When Patrick went public we received phone calls from Russia, Brisbane, Australia, the UK and around New Zealand from men who were sexually abused as vulnerable children at Maryland's (the name of the school run by the Order).

Darryl came to me with his parents when we set up a support system for those affected. With his help and the help of his parents we organized legal advice, a parents support group and a peer support group for survivors. Many are still in contact with us today and I have regular phone calls with Darryl and we still meet up on several occasions.

One of those occasions was in Wellington when Dame Susan Devoy organized a day in her role as Human Rights Commissioner to help put pressure on Government to hold a Royal Commission into the abuse of children in care.

Darryl played a part in this and for that and knowing his journey I was proud to sit with him. Darryl's life has not been easy yet he has managed to lift himself up away from being a victim sorted through his life as a survivor of horrendous sexual, physical and emotional abuse and is now a Navigator in control of his own life, who he wants to be and where he wants to go.

FORWARD

From Maryland's Christchurch St John of God Brothers aka Hospitaller Brothers Order of Saint John of God to Department of Social Welfare abuse as a State Ward at Campbell Park School & Stanmore Road Boys,then to Brisbane Australia and was made a state ward of Queensland and suffered more at Baptist Union of Queensland, who ran Talera Lodge Residential Home. And at Westbrook Training Centre and Wilson Youth Hospital and Crossroads,more in the so called care of the Department of Families, Queensland Government Australia to prison time to Rome Italy making a stand at the Vatican Summit on Child Sexual Abuse in 2019 for all New Zealanders who had been sexually abused by the Roman Catholic Church to face the Catholic Church head on at the Vatican.

Darryl is man of great courage who no longer stands back being told how things should be, and has taken control of his own life.

I am proud to call Darryl a friend and a colleague and admire not only what he is doing for himself but his ability to set an example for other male survivors of sexual trauma to follow.

I wish Darryl all the best in his continual journey in his healing and desire to be a better human being.

Ken Clearwater, Survivor & National Advocate

Male Survivors Aotearoa

MESSAGE FROM DUGAL AMOUR

Campbell Park is about a half hour drive 'up the valley' from Oamaru. I would have gone there about the same time as Darryl was there, helping my Dad repair the slates on the turrets of the 'castle'. Over the years I had been back to look at potential restoration projects and attended the 'Taste of Waitaki' event, front-lined by Peter Gordon and show -casing the best of the Waitaki culinary produce and art.

My memories appear in complete contrast to what Darryl and many other boys experienced over the 80 year period that Campbell Park operated as an institution for 'disadvantaged boys'.

Yet it is this juncture that is so critical to survivors. Facing the denial from those, willing to break the comfort of their own perceptions. "They were such nice people', "I had the perfect childhood", "That could have never happened".

This makes Darryl all more extraordinary. Not only has he survived such unthinkable atrocities as a child and throughout his life but with singular determination he has pushed through the constant barrage of denial and challenges, to tell the truth.

To shine a light on those dark places people do not want to see and ultimately to bring an awareness so that these atrocities happened no more.

Dugal Armour, Survivor

Male Survivors Otago

MESSAGE FROM TONE MILLER

I have been Darryl's Intensional Peer Support worker for some years now. It has been a pleasure watching Darryl grow in so many ways.

He does not let his past hold him back but uses it to find strength and encourage others to do the same.

Even at times when his life was more of a struggle he finds the determination to keep moving forward.

When telling his story he shows the courage and kindness of a man who recognises his hurt yet shares so that others can know they are not alone.

I am proud of Darryl for the work he does and more so to call him a friend and a brother.

Tone Miller

Peer Support Worker

Male Survivors Otago

CONTENTS

CONTENTS

CONTENTS

CONTENTS

1972 AFTER MARYLANDS

Things got real bad for me I started getting into trouble in a big way.

And my parents had no idea that I had been badly sexually abused by Brother Rodger William MOLONEY Prior of Maryland's School in Halwell, Christchurch. But told them and got a hidding for lieing.

And I was 7 or 8 years old in November and I thought I was older and that had a lot going on in my head even then and started to live in a world of my own to get away from the truth that the Brothers of the Hospitaller Order of Saint John of God (Saint John of God Brothers) sexually abused me and some of the older boys of Maryland's School sexually abused me alone.

My mother didn't know how to handle me and she thought it was her fault I was acting like this and it wasn't her fault or my father's it was evil people stating they were for God but instead would turn to the boys of Maryland's and rape them.

I couldn't stay in school and my parents were at an end with it

1973 RICCARTON SCHOOL

In 1973 I was in school at Riccarton and meet my school teacher who was a god send but I didn't know that for years later. When I was in her class I was in the school Drama group and loved it.

I was I had keep it up and this is where I meet my best friend Paul Farbe and some of the classmates were just friends.

I wish I had told my teacher than of the abuse at Maryland's but I throught noone would believe me and so I acted out instead. Mrs Martin was a good teacher and she had this little car and she would take as kids on outings and to plays we acted in at different schools and even got a shock and acted in a play at my old school Maryland's and hated being there.

1973 TEMPLETON HOSPITAL

March 1973 my parents we were living near Hornby, Christchurch at the time and my mother was just about to go into hospital to have my sister.

And I was pack off to Templeton Hospital a week before the baby was born and I was allowed to go to school at Riccarton School because my parents ask for me to keeping on doing this.

I was sexually abused there is the kitchen back roon where an old guy use to sleep.

JOURNEY TO CAMPBELL PARK SCHOOL 1975

We were all meet at the buses going down to Oamaru way with social workers and heaps of others boys going to Campbell Park School, Kurow, Otago, and we were leaving from Christchurch my home town where I was born.

The buses were full of boys from all ages some the same age has me and some younger and some a lot older.

There were three buses in total and the boys were from all of New Zealand the boy sitting next to me was from Taupo and I ask him were that was and he stated me that I must be dumb and from the South Island. Because most people knew were Taupo was. The colour of the buses where white and blue a funny colour for school buses. I find out they were not school buses. The Department of Education had chartered the buses from a company.

Some of the boys were from Auckland, Hamilton, Napier, Hastings and Dunedin, even close to home in Oamaru.

We stop for lunch near a river and than went on to the Kurow pass turn off. And I was told by a social welfare worker on the bus not long now and we will be at Campbell Park School.

ARRIVING AT CAMPBELL PARK SCHOOL

Arriving at Campbell Park School on the 22 of May 1975 where we got off the buses and had some dinner and than was told to wait in the dinning room so we can be put into the right house. I was only 10 years old at the time and was told I was going to Taylor House along with some of the boys I meet on the bus. And has I remember it was for the younger boys Taylor House from 5 years to 12 years old. When you turned 13 years you went on to Dansey House for boys of 13 years to 15 years and than on to Campbell House for boys who were 16 years to 18 years old.

The abuse started the first night at Taylor House by one of the boys thinking I was a toilet and piss into my mouth when I was asleep and I ask him why and stated I was his bitch to fuck anytime he wanted and he was from Campbell House and around about 16 years old and I was only 10 years old at time.

And so he rape me the first night I was the hell hole of Campbell Park School and he told me no one will believe me because he was an older boy and I had just got there and I was making trouble if I had said something.

So this older boy would come to Taylor House once a month and would wake me up and take me to the outside toilet area and rape me and sometimes when I was upset I would hid in the bush across from Taylor House and he would find me and rape me some more.

ARRIVING AT CAMPBELL PARK SCHOOL

One night in June it was a cold night and some of the older boys from Dansey House came down to Taylor House that was next door and physically made me sick when they made me watch has five older boys gang rape a 7 year old boy who they hatred.

And I was told not to say a thing and it is the first time I have spoken about in 48 years or so. At night was a bad time at Taylor House if it wasn't the older boys raping you, it was the night watchman.

It was my second day at the school and it was very crazy place a lot of the bigger boys would rape you at night and pick on you at school.

There was a bit of a rule that I find out about later on if you a small boy or easy boy to pick on you would get it at school by the older and bigger boys, rape at night.

The staff didn't about you even after you made a complaint about it and they want there turn with you.

JASON KIU AN OLDER BOY

When I was in Dansey House at the age of 13 years or 14 years I first ran into Jason Kiu and it was the first time I was in A group and was allowed to stay up late to watch TV and the boys from C & D, B groups had gone to bed and Jason stated to me that he like younger boys that were just growing there hair below.

I didn't understand him.

He stated he wanted to play with me and I stated no I am not into other boys or men I am not gay I am into women. And that is when he told me that I was his bitch in the dormitory and he will come and visit at night and when we are on camping trips he stated he will have me in his tent.

I was very upset at this and he told me to never tell anyone about it. I ask him why is because I am easy and all the older guys go for little white boys to fuck.

Early one morning I awoke to find Jason on top of me having sex with me and that was rape and I was made to lay in my bed with his hand over my mouth so I don't say a thing.

He made me do oral sex on him and he made me sick.

I watch him rape Wayne Humphreys a friend of mine.

And then he was after other boys I was told by a friend of Jason that he was doing this to me and others because it happened to him. What a fucking joke.

Mrs D Johnson School Teacher & her husband

Mrs Johnson in 1976 was my room 4 teacher and was ok at first and was a bitch who would keep me back in class to have her fun has she put it.

Mrs Johnson first told me that she knew how to make bad boys do the right thing and be quiet in class. She made me to do oral sex on her into be sex.

And once a week she would keep me back for lessons has she told my house masters and he would make me an 13 year old handicap have sex with her. And she told me never to tell anyone or she would make me sleep at night up at the grave yard where they eat teenage boys and I had nightmares for years of that.

When her and her husband were in change of me to take me to Dunedin Hospital for appoints over me having an operation on my nose they would take me to their place in the Village and take turns with me to have sick with.

The husband Mr Johnson was also house master at Taylor House and was going around at night to some of the boys beds and sexually abusing them why they sleep and I woken up when he was doing it to me

She was pure evil to me and would send me to Mr O'Connor's to get hit by him and she would enjoy sending me to him for doing nothing.

When I was in the care of Mr Johnson who was a house master I was taken to a shed and physcially and sexually abused by him and one day he got me in the garden and played with my penis.

It was night and it was late at night and I was in my dormitory and was woken up by kissing me all over and this was a sick thing to do to any child.

When Mr Johnson was killed at Lake Benmore along with another staff member on a boat along with her son. I was only unhappy that her son died he was a good person and a friend.

Stanmore Road Boys Home , Christchurch

In 1974 I first went to Stanmore Road Boys Home and the first night there I was rape by four older boys and I was only 9 years old at the time and started running away from there after that. I was already made a state ward by the Nelson Children's Court. We lived in Jenner Road then.

I was place in the kitchen by two very nice ladies who worked in the kitchen to get me away from some of the older boys who were bully's.

I was sent to Moray Street Family Home on the 5th of April 1974 in Christchurch were I was placed by the Department of Social Welfare were I was physically abused by my foster mother a Mrs Barry from a file note dated 10th of April 1974 on my personal file in which the social worker expressed concern Mrs Barry's harsh response to me when I was returned after running away. She also commented that you (me) were obviously afraid of Mrs Barry. The senior social worker instructed the social worker to follow this up with Mrs Barry but because the files are missing I couldn't tell if this happened.

By 1974 I was a Campbell Park School were more hell started for me. Stanmore Road Boys Home was used alot of the time for me in 1977 to 1978 when I was at school at Campbell Park.

In 1977 December I meet Christopher Truscott and we were told the ones that were there for Christmas had to go on this camp to Okains Bay at the school there and they were very mean to use and made has bath in the schools swimming pool and the staff didn't do that.

It was bad at night Mr Barnden and Miss Martin don't care about want the others boys were doing to me and Chris at night and they were only a few feet away from the abuse and let it happen. And Michael Edwards and Darryl Fraser was there and they were part of the bully's at Stanmore Road Boys Home and they rape me and Chris, the staff did nothing.

Mr Medcalf House master

Mr Medcalf wife who work in the offices of the school complex and she was very nice to me but on the other hand her husband was very cruel and would me do oral sex on him.

Mr Medcalf was also having raping alot of the younger boys

like Barry Allan Ryder and he was the

youngest boy in the entire school.

Over the time I was at Campbell Park this monster rape me on a number of occasions and sometimes I was told he will kill my entire family. And he told me that my parents didn't care because I was a state ward and he can do want he wish with me and even kill me if he wishes and he stated that raping me is more fun.

Campbell House (Older boys of Campbell Park School)

Campbell House is where we were made to go to Church groups where a lot has hatred and we were made to do oral sex on the older boys in the toilet when they caught has away from the church group I can remember them telling the house masters to fuck off or they will kill them and they did has they were told.

This is were the staff growned a lot of the older boys to become something they are not I think.

Mr Terry Mathers House Master of Dansey House

This housemaster like his job upsetting me and making me do more work around the Dansey House and I couldn't believe it because I had done nothing to him.

He one day was working the 3 to 10pm shift of the house and head house master on that evening and he was mine house master and he called me into his office after me and two of my mates were playing rockets and he just wanted to punish me and the others so he got the leather belt out of the draw and give me and my friends six of the best for doing nothing but playing rockets we had toy rockets and we were playing that we imagine we would go to the moon to get away from that hell hole.

Mathers had rape me in the office one night and blamed this on one of the other boys and punish me and the other boys for his sexually raping me in my bed that night. How sick is that?

Mr Terry Mathers House Master of Dansey House

This monster would prey on the boys after bedtime.

I was in his care after I hurt my leg and I could get to the lounge very slowly walking and so my meals were brought to me. My parents were in Australia when this was going on.

The day it happened I was in the lounge and Mr Mathers stated to me to get my pants down because I had been a bad boy and I told I wasn't bad boy that I wasn't getting my pants down an he hit me in the head and told me to fucking do has I was told or he will let the older boys in the House rape me again.

I stated WANT THE FUCK!

I told him to go and fuck himself and leave me alone and I am only a kid. And he stated a boy that he can happy with has make his he like.

Anyway he stated we were going for a ride in his car. And he pick me up and put me in the seat beside him and he drove the car outside the grounds of the school and I told him that we need to go back to the school otherwise I will be in trouble they will say I run away. And stated I was with a staff member and that is OK. And I laugh and he hit for that by now we were near the Benmore Lake and he told me to get everything off this time and he wants to kiss me all over and stated FUCK OFF MATE YOU SICK FUCK and he hit me hard with his foot and told me to do it or else he will kill me.

I did what he said. And he told me to put my clothes back on and get back into the car and so I did and he told me to give him a blow job and I told him to get fuck. And stated you must remember by now you are my property you little shit so do has you are fucking told. So I was made to do oral sex on this MONSTER in the back of his car and this happened to a lot by this monster.

Mr P.R. Parsons House Master Dansey House

The time Mr Parsons had come along at Dansey House I was been rape by staff and older boys a lot and they was happening daily.

The Survival of the Bush has he put it

Mr Parsons wasn't a nice man he was an cunt to put in nice words and nothing I did was right.
And he would take me away from Dansey House at Night and take me to the bushes across the road from Dansey House and make me do oral sex on him.

His survival plan for the boys of Dansey House was to make has strong has he put it to me was that we needed to have sex with him.

I thought he was crazy and I told him I wasn't going to do that and he told me to I was in his care and care of the State and he can do what he wanted with me at anytime I was the property of the Crown and he worked for the Crown so he can do it.

I told him I was going to tell my parents and he stated that they will not believe you because you are known for lieing and that was because I was telling the truth and no one believed me.

So he keep on taking me away at night to the bushes across the road from Dansey House to make me do oral sex on him and he rape me there also.

P.G. Aspden, Supertindent of the Complex and School

Mr Aspden was after my mother's stamp collection but to get it he wanted me to sign them over to him to sell and put the money into a trust fund for me and I didn't believe him because I told my mother give them to me before they left for Christchurch in November 1977 just after my 14th birthday on the 11th of November.

And called him a lier and he hit me for that.

He told me he could make my life more hell than what it is now if I didn't sign over the rights to the Stamp Collections and I told him to go and fuck himself. He told me that he will let the other boys fuck me and I told the fucker that was already going on and he surprise me when he told me that he was allowing this to happen because he didn't like me.

I told him I will make a complaint to my social worker about this and he laugh and said who will believe you. You lie to much.

I told him I would run away.

He stated we will give you a pack laugh to take with you and I laugh and stated that is not running away that is a day outing.

The Stamp Collection was safe because I ask my social worker who didn't work at Campbell Park School to keep an eye on it.

The Cave of Hell

The Cave was behind Campbell House were the older boys would go and smoke, and rape the younger boys they would find or get outside doing yard work.

One day I was working in the kitchen, first in the kitchen has a dishwasher and than working in the dinning room has a cleaner. That was Ok I think.

I went for a walk for a break and didn't know about the cave of hell into I was walking pass it and happy looking at the blue sky and one of the bigger and older boys came out of the cave with some of his mates from Campbell House they worked on the farm or where ever.

They got around me and told me to come with them and I told them that I had to get back to the dinning room and finish my job and I was surprise to see the cook with them and told me not to worry about that because they were now going to have their fun.

I told them to all go and get fuck. With them was Jason Kiu and I fight them but lost and I wasn't very good at fighting.

But one of the boys got me in a headlock and I said fuck off cunt and they told me that is what they wanted to fuck my cunt. I told them I am not a woman and didn't have one and they stated that is want my bum is for.

And they put this cloth in my month and they tided down and was rape by this fat hairy cook who worked in the kitchen and than the other boys from Campbell House had a go and they all wanted there turn.

I was let go on the grounds never to speak about this to anyone and it is the first time I have speak about it because it still gives me nightmares.

The Grave Yard

It was a bad night in my dormitory because they keep on coming I was in my bed and the older boys from Dansey and Campbell were in Taylor House for the younger boys and this was my second week into been at Campbell Park School and we the new ones were taken up to the Grave Yard and told by the older boys of Dansey and Campbell Houses that it was the night when the older boys have there fun.

I stated that I will tell the staff and the night watchman come out behind the grave and stated they will not listen to me because just about every staff member at the school was sexually & physcially abusing the boys there.

And the night watchman caught me after I moved towards a tree and made me get on and lay on the ground he told me and he started to remove my clothes with his hands and he told me to kiss him and I told him to get fuck you mother fucker.

And he hit me in the mouth and told me to give him a blow job and stated I wasn't a woman and he stated the older boys here and the staff at the school will make me into their bitch.

So I was rape that night at the Grave Yard by six older boys and the night watchman.

The Flying Fox Area

Out of Bounds but the older boys would take the younger boys and the boys that were easy to rape to this place.

I was one of the weaker boys at Campbell Park School and they all knew it and was a target the minute I arrived at the school.

The Gym

The Gym was never safe for any of the younger boys because this is were some of the staff would take you for there re education of you has they put it.

I played up and I was taken there by three older boys and they started Darryl from Taylor House and they were from Campbell House I was only 11 years old at the time and they were at least 16 or 17 years old.

I was told the staff wish to re educate me and the three older boys were going to have their turn with me. I told them to go and get fuck and I was told that was going to happen to me.

Eric Smith was at the Gym with two other boys and I was just coming back from having a walk from the far away Rugby field because I wish to be by myself. Eric Smith and two other boys got me behind the gym and tired me to a tree and rape me.

Swimming Pool & Changing room

The Charging rooms were lockable and the older boys would love to lock use in there and rape has one by one.

Sometimes they would rape has in the pool itself why the staff were watching.

Abuse at the hall at night

This hall is were we would go there after breakfast in the morning and Mr Aspden talk about want had been happening over the weekend or the week or talk about end of term.

And would be telling us who was off prives for not behaving and I would think to myself. Who didn't let me rape him or give him oral sex.

The hall at night was another story of hell for me. I was taken there one day at midnight by the night watchman and he had the key and unlocked the door and told me to lay on the large chair and get my pants off because he was going to fuck me and I told him to fuck off and he hit me and hit me into I gave in. And he made me do oral sex on him into I was sick and made me clean up that mass also.

Abuse at Dansey Hut

When I use to go there during the day it was OK sometimes but when I would be taken there are night in pyjamas by a staff member or two and made to do oral sex on them and then rape me and that was very upsetting for me. And still get nightmares from it now.

The Castle of Abuse

Every night I was at Campbell Park School I was taken there by an older boy who had a keys to the Castle and would meet up with three or sometimes four older boys from Campbell House and sometimes they would bring a new boy from Taylor House to be rape and beaten has part of a game to the older boys.

I ask one night why do they have the keys to the Castle and they told me the head of the complex Mr Aspden give them to him and the others so they can have there fun and Mr Aspden one night came to see what they were doing to me and this new boy from Taylor House and stated it is my turn to have fun now.

I don't think even his wife knew what he did to some of the boys in his care.

One night three younger boys and six older boys and ten staff members were in the Castle taking the turn of me and two other younger boys and it would and I was a State Ward in the Care of the Director-General of the Department of Social Welfare and they didn't care what the animals were doing to me and other boys in the Castle or any where at Campbell Park.

And if they knew they didn't give a fuck.

I remember very well the hell I was put though at the Castle at night times and A lot of boys from this school would remember themselves been a victim here.

Mr O 'Connor Teacher abuser

Mr O'Connor was the owner of a farm near to Kurow, Otago at the time he was teaching me at Campbell Park School. He wasn't a nice man and he was a fun of physcial abuse on the boys and he was hatred by all the students.

After one night one of the young boys was having problems with his reading he keep him after class for a long time and it wasn't normal for Mr O'Connor to keep any boy back after class he was a teacher and a man to get home to his daughter and wife and to the small farm and his old car collection.

This boy was my friend and he was in my dorm and want ever happened to him was sad to hear after he went home for school holidays he was find dead with a rope around his neck and he hung himself because something that happened at school the note stated. His mother sent to me when I was in Australia.

What did Mr O'Connor do to make this boy kill himself. A lot of questions come into my head over the years. Was Mr O'Connor raping him? We will never know.

Only the boy and Mr O'Connor know the truth and why did Mr O'Connor go all quiet when we use to stay the boys name.

Mr O'Connor was a bad man he was acting like he was a god in the classroom and we could not do anything about it.

Dunedin Hospital for me

Me at Dunedin Hospital in 1974 on my 11th Birthday.

First I had to have an operation to clear my nose after I had a fallen when I was three years old left me not breathing from my nose and I had to be in hospital because I had a broke down from the abuse at Campbell Park School and no one knew about it.

Peter Holdem Like the younger boys

Peter Holdem was at Campbell Park School I was there and he first preyed on me in Waiau and than at Campbell Park School. He told me that if I tell anyone like the staff, teachers or other boys he would kill me.

So he would come to my dorm late at night and get me out of bed and go to the outside toilet area that was out of bounds at night.

And he would get me into the toilet area and lock the room the toilet door and make me do oral sex on him and also than he would rape me and he than would say he would see me tomorrow night.

Peter than got one night brought a mate with him from Campbell House and they would take their turn with me and I was rape by them into the early hours of the next morning.

I was saw and couldn't walk very well and told the house master in the morning I wasn't feeling very well and they believed me and I was given bed rest and I was on bed rest for two days,

I told matron that I wasn't feeling very well.

And I remembered want Peter had stated me to me if I stated anything he would kill me.

He was always hanging around the school toilets to get some young boy.

One day I was going to met another teacher in the staff for my spelling class one to one and he told me to get the one to one spelling finish and make up that I have to got to the toilet and he rape me in the toilet.

Working at the Kitchen at the School

It was never that nice. I was a kitchen hand at first and one of the guys in the

dinning room wanted to have a change and I agreed with him and we ask the head cook and stated it was ok. So we did and I started working in the dinning room and a Mr Wearing would come in a lot and told me he was going to have me transfered to work with my on the farm and the staff stated that I couldn't I was too young because I was still at school and so I told him to get fuck.

He was a very nasty person he was always in my face when I was back at Taylor House and when I was in Dansey House the same thing. We hatred each other.

One day he made me run up and down a hill at the back of Dansey House along with a Mr Shakespeare because he wanted to make me unhappy and he told me there was a bush there and force me into it and got me to do oral sex on him.

Eric Smith Would rape me daily (And the staff knew)

Eric Smith (no relation to me) was raping me every chance he got. I wasn't safe from him and he was very fit and would hit me a lot and told me to do oral sex on him and I had to do has I was told into I was sick.

I was never told by staff at the School or anyone that Eric Smith like young boys or boys who were handicap.

FEEDBACK MEETING ON THE ABUSE IN STATE CARE

Feedback Meeting 13 December 2011 Darryl Smith b 11.11.1963

Summary of Findings

Sexual assaults and bullying by other boys at Campbell Park

1. You named Eric Smith and Jason Kiu as having sexually abused you as well as other boys whose names you couldn't remember. Records show that you were sexually assaulted, bullied and physically attacked by other boys soon after you arrived at Campbell Park until you left. The descriptions you gave about how and where this happened to you is supported by information I found on records about the behaviour of some of the boys. There was clear information that Eric Smith had sexually assaulted you on a number of occasions and that staff were aware of this but unable to stop this behaviour. There are records that other boys also sexually abused you and that on some occasions you were both strapped for this behaviour.

2. There is a lot of evidence that you were constantly bullied by other boys through out the time you were at Campbell Park. It appears that little was done by staff to provide protection for you rather it was believed that you had brought this on yourself and that because you couldn't defend yourself that was your fault.

Physical abuse by staff at Campbell Park

3. While corporal punishment was still legal during the 1970s some of the staff members named by you had been reported by their colleagues for harshly treating other boys at Campbell Park. We accept that it is likely that they treated you the same way. As you know from your files these people also made negative and disparaging comments about you.

Sexual assaults by staff at Campbell Park

4. While there is nothing on file to support your claims that staff at Campbell Park sexually abused you, the Police have recently confirmed that Mr Mathers was convicted in 1984 of 5 sexual abuse charges. We have accepted that it is more likely than not that Mr Mather's sexually abused you.

Emotional abuse

5. The comments written about you by staff were consistently and universally unkind. We believe it is more likely than not that your emotional needs were not met while you were at Campbell Park.

6. We also note that although you had told people at Campbell Park that you had problems with your sight, that you were not believed and that medical checks showed you had normal sight however when the Stanmore Rd staff later sent you in April 1977 to an eye specialist he confirmed that you had lost most of the sight in your right eye. This was not able to be remedied.

Discharge from Campbell Park in 1978

7. You should not have been discharged back home in 1978. The Nelson DSW office, did not agree neither did the local educational psychologist as they thought it was too soon and that your mother would not be able to cope. The process set out to be followed when there were disagreements between the institution and

FEEDBACK MEETING ON THE ABUSE IN STATE CARE

local office were not followed. Early in 1977 you were running away again and an urgent recommendation was made for you to return to Campbell Park but it took a whole term for you to be readmitted. It took sometime for you to catch up with where you had been with your school work when you went back to Campbell Park.

8. Issues re Stanmore Road

9. At the time of your first admission in 1974 the staff were obviously concerned for your well being and demanded that you be removed and placed in a more suitable environment. At this time Stanmore Rd was overcrowded with 31 boys when there should have been only 24. You went to an aunt for Easter and then placed in the Moray Avenue Family Home in Dunedin.

10. Stanmore Rd also queried the suitability of your second placement noting that the Boys' Home was overcrowded and under pressure with remand cases from the court. As there were no other placements available you stayed at Stanmore Rd and attended school there until you went to Campbell Park. Although it was noted that you tended to wander off your behaviour during this time was described as "good."

11. Between 1977 and 1978 you spent school holidays at Stanmore Rd as your parents had gone to Australia and no family members were prepared to have you stay with them. Stanmore Rd staff were aware that this wasn't the best place for you but as you always ran away from other placements and your family wouldn't have you to stay with them there were no other options.

Sexual abuse at Stanmore Rd

12. You have said in your statement of claim, in the interview and in subsequent conversations that Steven Crees raped you on a number of occasions at Stanmore Road. We have not been able to find information on any files about this.

Secure care at Stanmore Road

13. You said in your statement of claim that you were placed in secure at Stanmore Rd for up to a month at a time for running away.

14. I could find only 1 record of you ever being in secure care and that was for 3 hours on the 28th April 1979 after you had run away for 45 minutes. You had been placed in Stanmore Rd by the police on a warrant on the 18th April after you had come back to NZ from Australia. You were returned to Australia on the 14th May 1979

Physical abuse at the Tahananui Family Home Nelson

15. In your statement of claim you say that Mr Heath beat you and would lock you in a closet for up to 2 hours at a time. You also said that he raped you and forced you to perform oral sex on him. You also said that the Strawbridges physically abused you when they were the family home foster parents.

16. A file note for the 36d March 1977 states that you seemed happy and settled with the Heaths. I couldn't find any complaints about the Heaths or the Strawbridges. Both sets of foster parents were seen as being good foster

FEEDBACK MEETING ON THE ABUSE IN STATE CARE

parents, and this view is supported by talking to people who knew them at this time.

Physical abuse at the Dunedin Moray Place Family Home

17. In your statement of claim you say that Mrs Barry physically assaulted you. The foster files for Mr and Mrs Barry have not been able to be found neither has the Moray Place Family Home file. There is a file note for the 10th April 1974 on your personal file in which the social worker expressed concern at Mrs Barry's harsh response to you when you were returned after running away. She also commented that you were obviously afraid of Mrs Barry. The senior social worker instructed the social worker to follow this up with Mrs Barry but because the files are missing I couldn't tell if this happened.

Other concerns

18. Schooling

When you were at Campbell Park you attended school regularly and your education file shows that you had a special work programme. There are school reports and examples of your work on this file. It would be good for you to ask for a copy of the file to be sent to you. When you at Stanmore Rd during term time you also went to school there.

19. Life skills

When you were at Campbell Park you were expected to take care of yourself, make your bed, keep your room tidy etc. You also learnt other skills such as woodwork, helping in the kitchen and so on.

Darryl we are really sorry that you were not kept safe when you were at Campbell Park and that these things happened to you. They should not have happened.

Judy Moore
Senior Social Work Advisor
13 December 2011

TIMELINE OF STATE CARE ABUSE

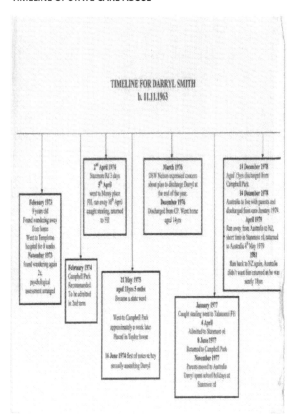

SONJA COOPER LAWYER LETTER

Sonja M. Cooper

BARRISTER & SOLICITOR

Level 1
Gleneagles Building
69-71 The Terrace
Wellington 6143
PO Box 10899
The Terrace
Telephone: 04-4989025
Fax: 04-4994299
Email: sonjallawcooper@xtra.co.nz

S M Cooper
19 November 2007

Darryl Smith
33 Kana Street
Motaura
Southland
INVERCARGILL

Dear Darryl

FORWARDING OF MAIL

I refer to our communications with you.

I have received a letter from Grant Simon, addressed to you. I have now **enclosed** that letter.

I am happy to be the "middleman" for this initial correspondence, but any further communications between you and Grant in future will need to be done directly. Unfortunately, we do not have the time or the resources to facilitate forwarding mail to our clients from people outside this office.

I hope all is well with you.

Yours sincerely

Sonja M Cooper

MINISTRY OF EDUCATION LETTERS

MINISTRY OF EDUCATION
Te Tāhuhu o te Mātauranga

26 September 2007   National Office   45-47 Pipitea Street   Phone: 0-4-463 8188
    Thorndon   Fax: 0-4-463 8373
    PO Box 1666   www.minedu.govt.nz
    Wellington
    New Zealand

Mr D.W. Smith
33 Kana Street
Mataura
Southland

Dear Mr Smith

I am replying to your updated letter to me, which I received on 27 August 2007, about Campbell Park School.

You state that you are writing a book about Campbell Park School and you have asked whether or not the ministry might be interested in stopping the writing and publishing of the book by giving you compensation, and also buying the rights for the book.

In relation to the book, the ministry does not wish to buy the rights, nor do we wish to stop you writing or publishing your work. Within the normal constraints of the law in the publishing area you are free to do so.

On the matter of compensation I have referred your letter (and this reply) to the Crown Law Office who are handling your claim relating to Campbell Park School on the Ministry's behalf. They will discuss your claim, as you suggest, with your lawyer, Ms Cooper.

Yours sincerely

Jan Breakwell
Chief Legal Advisor

MINISTRY OF EDUCATION LETTERS

MINISTRY OF EDUCATION
Te Tāhuhu o te Mātauranga

Ministry of Education
National Office
P O Box 1666
Wellington
New Zealand

Legal Services Division
Phone 04 463 8095
Fax 463 8779

4 March 2004

Darryl W Smith
Private Bag 3000
WANGANUI

Dear Darryl Smith

The letter you wrote to the Christchurch office of the Ministry of Education has been referred to me. I note that the Ministry will be conducted by your lawyer next year.

Yours sincerely

Jan Breakwell
Manager Legal Services

MINISTRY OF EDUCATION LETTERS

MINISTRY OF EDUCATION

12 February 2003

Darryl Smith
Private Bag 4726
Templeton
CHRISTCHURCH

Dear Darryl Smith

I am replying to your letter of 31 December 2002 which went to the Ministry's Christchurch office and was referred by them to me. In your letter you repeated allegations you had made in a previous letter to the Ministry, about Campbell Park Boys School, and you give some details about named staff at the former school.

As you will appreciate, allegations such as the ones you have made are very serious and take time to consider. You have said in your letters that you seek compensation by way of an out of court settlement. The Ministry is not able to consider such compensation until a process of establishing a cause of action, establishing damage and eligibility, and verifying (as much as is possible) background facts, has been gone through.

You will need to seek expert advice to formulate your allegations (which are still too general) into a claim which the Ministry can proceed to investigate. Please ask your lawyer to correspond directly with me as I will be handling the matter from now on.

Yours sincerely

Ian Brookwell
Manager Legal Services

MINISTRY OF EDUCATION LETTERS

MINISTRY OF EDUCATION
Te Tāhuhu o te Mātauranga

17 February 2003

National Office

Legal Services Division
45-47 Pipitea Street
Thorndon
PO Box 1666
Wellington
New Zealand

Phone: 0-4-463 8645
Direct: 463 8186
Fax: 463 8776
www.minedu.govt.nz

Patrick McPherson
Grant Cameron Associates
P O Box 3241
CHRISTCHURCH

Dear Patrick McPherson

Darryl W Smith – Allegations of abuse in relation to the former Campbell Park Boys School

I understand that you are acting for Darryl Smith in relation to another matter, and that you may be acting for him in respect of some allegations of sexual and other abuse arising from his time at the former Campbell Park Boys School.

I attach a recent letter that I sent to Mr Smith and I advise that he has informed the Ministry that you are to be his contact point from now on. I expect that I will hear from you in due course.

Yours sincerely

Ian Breakwell
Manager Legal Services

MINISTRY OF EDUCATION LETTERS

17 February 2003

National Office

Legal Services Division
45-47 Pipitea Street
Thorndon
PO Box 1666
Wellington
New Zealand

Phone: 0-4-463 8000
Direct: 463 8188
Fax: 463 8719
www.minedu.govt.nz

Patrick McPherson
Grant Cameron Associates
P O Box 3241
CHRISTCHURCH

Dear Patrick McPherson

Darryl W Smith – Allegations of abuse in relation to the former Campbell Park Boys School

I understand that you are acting for Darryl Smith in relation to another matter, and that you may be acting for him in respect of some allegations of sexual and other abuse arising from his time at the former Campbell Park Boys School.

I attach a recent letter that I sent to Mr Smith and I advise that he has informed the Ministry that you are to be his contact point from now on. I expect that I will hear from you in due course.

Yours sincerely

Jan Breakwell
Manager Legal Services

MINISTRY OF EDUCATION LETTERS

12 February 2003

National Office

Legal Services Division
45-47 Pipitea Street
Thorndon
PO Box 1666
Wellington
New Zealand

Phone: 0-4-463 8000
DDisc: 463 8188
Fax: 463 8779
www.minedu.govt.nz

Darryl Smith
Private Bag 4726
Templeton
CHRISTCHURCH

Dear Darryl Smith

I am replying to your letter of 21 December 2002 which went to the Ministry's Christchurch office and was referred by them to me. In your letter you repeated allegations you had made in a previous letter to the Ministry, about Campbell Park Boys School, and you give some details about named staff at the former school.

As you will appreciate, allegations such as the ones you have made are very serious and take time to consider. You have said in your letters that you seek compensation by way of an out of court settlement. The Ministry is not able to consider such compensation until a process of establishing a cause of action, establishing damage and eligibility, and verifying (as much as is possible) background facts, has been gone through.

You will need to seek expert advice to formulate your allegations (which are still too general) into a claim which the Ministry can proceed to investigate. Please ask your lawyer to correspond directly with me as I will be handling the matter from now on.

Yours sincerely

Jan Breakwell
Manager Legal Services

MINISTRY OF EDUCATION LETTERS

MINISTRY OF EDUCATION
Te Tāhuhu o te Mātauranga

National Office

National Operations
45-47 Pipitea Street
Thorndon
PO Box 1666
Wellington
New Zealand

Phone: 0-4-463 8000
Direct: 463 8235
Fax: 0-4-463 8001
www.minedu.govt.nz

CEO 1119 (2)

29 December 2002

Darryl Smith
26 Bournemouth Crescent
Aranui
Christchurch

Dear Darryl

Nga mihi nui ki a koe. Greetings

I am writing to you about your letter of 22 November 2002. In that letter you have made allegations that you were sexually abused at Campbell Park Boys School, Otago. You have also made allegations about Stanmore Road Boys Home, family homes and Marylands. In your letter you seek compensation from the Crown.

These are disturbing matters for all concerned and raise many complex legal and historical factual issues. You need to seek the advice and assistance of a lawyer to proceed with your claims. You should also seek support for your own well-being if you have not already done so.

In order to respond properly to your general allegations, the Ministry needs more information. This should be in a more formal and detailed form and a lawyer can assist you with this. A more detailed claim should include specific information about dates, places, people, and events. It would also help if you stated on what basis you believe the Crown is liable.

While I am not able to assist you as you might have expected at this stage I can assure you that allegations such as the ones you have made are taken seriously. However, you have not yet provided enough information to enable a formal process to begin.

In relation to the allegations about Stanmore Road Boys Home and family homes. These may be better addressed to the Department of Child, Youth and Family Services, P O Box 2620, Wellington.

Yours sincerely
Naku noa, na

Kathy Phillips
Senior Manager
National Operations

MINISTRY OF EDUCATION LETTERS

MINISTRY OF EDUCATION
Te Tāhuhu o te Mātauranga

17 February 2003

National Office

Legal Services Division
45-47 Pipitea Street
Thorndon
P O Box 1666
Wellington
New Zealand

Phone 0-4-463 8000
Direct 463 8190
Fax: 463 8779
www.minedu.govt.nz

Patrick McPherson
Grant Cameron Associates
P O Box 3241
CHRISTCHURCH

Dear Patrick McPherson

Darryl W Smith – Allegations of abuse in relation to the former Campbell Park Boys School

I understand that you are acting for Darryl Smith in relation to another matter, and that you may be acting for him in respect of some allegations of sexual and other abuse arising from his time at the former Campbell Park Boys School.

I attach a recent letter that I sent to Mr Smith and I advise that he has informed the Ministry that you are to be his contact point from now on. I expect that I will hear from you in due course.

Yours sincerely

Ian Breakwell
Manager Legal Services

LETTER OF APOLOGY FOR THE ABUSE

MINISTRY OF SOCIAL DEVELOPMENT
Te Manatū Whakahiato Ora

2 9 JUN 2012

Bowen State Building, Bowen Street, Wellington 6011, PO Box 1556, Wellington 6140 • Telephone: 0-4-916 3300 • Facsimile: 0-4-918 0099

Mr Darryl Smith
C/- Cooper Legal
Barristers and Solicitors
PO Box 10899
The Terrace
WELLINGTON

Dear Mr Smith

This letter, and the other parts of the settlement, marks the end of a very long journey for you, but it also marks the beginning of what I know will be a very positive future.

I understand that you have faced a huge number of challenges in your life from an early age. You have been in care both in New Zealand and Australia and have endured experiences during those times that you should not have had to. Amongst the many New Zealand homes you spent time in I know that Campbell Park School stands out in your memory for many unfortunate reasons. The staff of the school had a responsibility to provide you with the care, safety and protection that you deserved. You were not always safe either from some of the staff or from some of the other pupils. Quite simply you were treated in a way that was not acceptable. I want to acknowledge that and as Chief Executive of the Ministry, formally and unreservedly apologise for all the wrongs that were done during the time you were in our care.

I have been amazed to learn of all that you have done in the past two years. The fact that you have been through so much, yet can still offer such meaningful support and understanding to others through your paintings says a huge amount about you as a person. I am really pleased that we are able to acknowledge all the good that your painting has done, through an additional payment that you can put towards art supplies.

Mr Young tells me that it is almost exactly 10 years since you first made contact with the Ministry to talk about your concerns. I am sorry that it has taken so long, but I am pleased that we are now at this point and I commend you for persevering and not giving up.

I trust that this letter of apology and the settlement payment provides you with acknowledgement of all the wrongs that were done and that you can look forward with a sense of achievement and of putting the past behind you.

I wish you all the very best.

Yours sincerely

Brendan Boyle
Chief Executive

 child, youth and family

 family community services

 STUDYLINK

 Work and Income

MEETINGS

MINISTRY OF SOCIAL DEVELOPMENT
Te Manatū Whakahiato Ora

National Office, Bowen State Building, Bowen Street, PO Box 1556, Wellington 6140 • Facsimile 0-4-915 0299

13 August 2010

Darryl Smith
Flat 5
31 Worcester Boulevard
CHRISTCHURCH 8013

Dear Darryl

As discussed and agreed, please find enclosed a copy of the written transcript of our 10 June 2010 meeting.

Every reasonable effort has been made to transcribe the meeting verbatim, but you may notice that there are some gaps denoted either by numbers and/or the word "inaudible". This has been done in those instances where it is not possible to hear or understand what is being said on the recording. The numbers denote the time point on the tape at which the speaker cannot be heard.

If you would like a copy of the audio tape itself (on CD) so you can compare it with the transcript, then please do not hesitate to ask.

If you have any other questions, please feel free to contact me on 04 916 9113 or on 0508 326 459.

Yours sincerely

Judy Moore
Senior Social Work Advisor
Care, Claims and Resolution

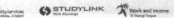

MINISTRY OF SOCIAL DEVELOPMENT
Te Manatū Whakahiato Ora

Bowen State Building, Bowen Street, Wellington 6011, PO Box 1556, Wellington 6140 • Facsimile: 0-4-918 0099

16 December 2011

Darryl Smith
80 Birchwood Rd
OHAI

Dear Darryl

This letter is a follow up to our meeting with you last week. I promised to send you details of how you can get your education files. You need to contact Dunedin Archives. The address is

Dunedin Regional Office556 George Street, Dunedin 9016, New Zealand
PO Box 6183, Dunedin North, Dunedin, New Zealand
Phone: (64-3) 477 0404
Fax: (64-3) 477 0422
E-mail: dunedin@archives.govt.nz

There are five records to request:-

Attendance Card - Darryl Smith CANB D227 / 4
Primary School Record - Darryl Smith CANB D227 / 8c
Individual Record - Darryl Smith 1969 -1978 CAJG D16 22547 Box 132

Personal file - Darryl Smith CAJG D16 63a 1976 /30
Personal file - Darryl Smith CAJG D16 64b 1978 /36

I have sent Cooper Legal a copy of the chronology and the feedback that I gave you.

Yours sincerely,

Judy Moore
Senior Social Work Advisor
Care, Claims and Resolutions

POEMS BY COLLEEN BOYD THAT MADE ME HAPPY

Hope

I feel in my heart that Hope is undermined and not given the consideration it deserves.

There are times when I get angry when I hear people's hopes get dashed by a person who thinks they have the right to tell these people that Hope is not real or needed or not to be believed in. Hope is a special thing that can come from the heart and that can be combined with something higher. It can give somebody that little bit extra until such a time that Hope is realized or given then a better quality of life.

When you take away a person's Hope you have the capability to break a person's spirit.

No one has the right to do that to anybody no matter how well intended their motives are. When you break a person's spirit you cause pain as much as any physical pain caused by a break. Hope is something that can get people to face their days when otherwise they would not even want to carry on or feel like no one believed in them to give them that edge in their lives.

When you give them something to work for or live for their smile that they may give you in return will light up your life for many years to come.

Put yourself in their shoes be it a child or even an animal they need something to look forward to. May people reconsider what they are going to say sometimes and think how they would feel in the same position.

Your blessings will be in the reality that you have put sunshine into a dark void in someone's life.

Kind regards,   Colleen Boyd

Soup

Soup to me can be a combination of many factors, there is soup of the day, where you can enjoy a variation on your favorite soup.

Then there is a recipe of life soup, ingredients are as follows; 1 large dollop of kindness, a dash of mystery, a handful of challenges, a spoonful of naughtiness, a large cupful of hopes and dreams, a smidgen of cheekiness and a helping of consideration and empathy.

Put it all together, stir with determination and strength and use it to keep the bad at bay and the spirit of the good, and the welcoming whispers of love in our ears that feels like a welcoming breeze on a hot day.

May my soup of life keep you filled with substantial goodness and health.

Bon apatite, enjoy life, but remember that there is my soup of life to turn to on a bad day.

By Colleen Boyd (your friend)

MORE INFORMATION ON PEOPLE WHO I HAVE ASK FOR HELP GRANT CAMEROON ASSOCATES

ASSOCIATES

BARRISTERS & SOLICITORS

1 March 2004

Mr Darryl Smith
Private Bag 3000
WANGANUI

Dear Darryl

VARIOUS MATTERS

1. We have received a number of items of correspondence from you recently regarding claims against the Government.

2. Darryl, we are not acting for you in relation to a claim against the New Zealand Government. We have no intention of proceeding with such a claim at this point in time. The firm simply does not have the resources given the ongoing claims against the Catholic Church to take on any class action of that kind.

3. We would suggest that you contact the New Zealand Law Society and try to find out whether or not any other solicitors are taking a class action against the Government at this time. Alternatively you could apply for legal aid.

Yours faithfully
GRANT CAMERON ASSOCIATES

Patrick McPherson
Associate

I:\Server\client\Order of St.John of God-712 Fellows-children\Smith, Darryl\01.26.02.04.cw.doc

letters
 # Ministry of Health
 # Ministry of child, Youth & family
& Ministry of Education.

GRANT ASHLEY CAMERON, LL B, FNZIM
MAURICE JOHN WALKER, LL B
ASSOCIATE: PATRICK JOHN MCPHERSON, LL B
LEVEL 8, FORSYTH BARR HOUSE, CNR COLOMBO & ARMAGH STS, CHRISTCHURCH
PHONE (03) 365-1347, FAX (03) 365-4599, N Z P O BOX 3641
Email grant.cameron@xtra.co.nz

RESEARCH AUTHORITY

I..Daniel William Smith.....grant authority to my lawyer, Sonja M Cooper, to release my contact details to Dr Elizabeth Stanley and/or David Cohen *(delete where applicable)* for the purposes of their research.

I also give permission for Dr Stanley and/or Mr Cohen *(delete where applicable)* to examine my files and records, which are held in my lawyer's office.

☑ This permission is given on the proviso that my name and contact details are kept confidential and are not to be used in any publication.

or

☐ I give permission for my details to be published.

(Tick whichever applies)

Signed _____

Dated   25/4/08

Legal Services
Agency
Pokapū Ratonga Ture

22 Mar 2010

Darryl William Smith
33 Kana Street
Mataura Southland 9753

Debt Management Group
PO Box 25324
Wellington 6146
DX SR38295
Freephone 0800 600 190
Facsimile 04 473 8829
Email debt@lsa.govt.nz

Dear Darryl William Smith

Request for more Information

   Your legal aid number is: 08063989

Thank you for your application for a write-off of your legal aid debt.

To assess your request, I need some more information:

- Please complete enclosed Statement of Financial Position form.
- Bank statements for the previous three months or a report from WINZ.
- Please provide documentation of your debts.
- Any other information you think may be useful to assess your file.

Please return this information to me as soon as you can, but no longer than four weeks from the date of this letter. After that time the Agency may proceed to make a decision based on the information on file.

Yours sincerely

Alexandra Nilova
Debt Officer

HELPING PEOPLE ACCESS JUSTICE

MORE LETTERS FROM THE MINISTRY OF SOCIAL DEVELOPMENT

MINISTRY OF SOCIAL DEVELOPMENT
Te Manatū Whakahiato Ora

Ministry of Social Development, Bowen State Building, Bowen Street 8691, PO Box 1556, Wellington 6140 • Telephone: 0-4-916 3300 • Facsimile: 0-4-918 0099

4 October 2010

Darryl Smith
Flat 6
31 Worcester Boulevard
CHRISTCHURCH 8013

Dear Darryl

As discussed today on the phone, please find enclosed a copy of two Campbell Park School magazines for 1975 and 1976. The 1976 magazine has a small article by you about your home town. I hope you find them interesting.

I hope your meeting with the City Mission went well and I know you will keep in touch and let me know when you shift and what your new address will be.

Take care and hope those aftershocks stop soon!!!

Yours sincerely

Judy Moore
Senior Social Work Advisor
Care, Claims and Resolution

  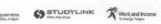

MINISTRY OF SOCIAL DEVELOPMENT
Te Manatū Whakahiato Ora

Ministry of Social Development, Bowen State Building, Bowen Street 6011, PO Box 1556, Wellington 6140
• Telephone 0-4-916 3300 • Facsimile 0-4-918 0099

28 October 2010

Darryl Smith
Flat 6
31 Worcester Boulevard
CHRISTCHURCH 8013

Dear Darryl

As discussed yesterday on the phone, here are some more Campbell Park magazines I have found for you. They are the Campbell Park magazines for 1977, 1978 and 1979. There is also a Dansey and Taylor House magazine for 1975. There is a group photo of you in the 1977 Campbell Park magazine. There is one of you also in the in the end of term school concert in the 1978 magazine.

I have enclosed a courier bag and some bubble wrap for the painting. We are all looking forward to seeing it and I will let you know when it arrives.

I hope your meeting with the people from the Ministry of Health has gone well.

Yours sincerely

Judy Moore
Senior Social Work Advisor
Care, Claims and Resolution

MINISTRY OF SOCIAL DEVELOPMENT
Te Manatū Whakahiato Ora

National Office, Bowen State Building, Bowen Street, PO Box 1556, Wellington 6140 • Facsimile 0-4-918 0099

14 May 2010

Mr Darryl Smith
145 Chesney Street
Tisbury
INVERCARGILL

Dear Darryl

This is to confirm our phone conversation of today's date.

You confirmed that you would like to meet with the Ministry directly in an effort to resolve your claim and I agreed that we were happy to make arrangements to do so.

I will have Fiona Wilson one of my senior advisors contact you directly to organise a time and place for the meeting. As also agreed, I will copy this letter to your solicitor Cooper Legal, for their information.

Yours sincerely

Garth Young
National Manager Care, Claims and Resolution

Cc

Cooper Legal
Barristers and Solicitors
PO Box 10899
The Terrace
WELLINGTON

MINISTRY OF SOCIAL DEVELOPMENT
Te Manatū Whakahiato Ora

Ministry of Social Development, Bowen State Building, Bowen Street, Wellington 6011, PO Box 1556, Wellington 6140 • Facsimile: 0-4-918 0099

4 June 2010

Darryl Smith
c/- Alpine View Holiday Park
650 Main South Road
Templeton
CHRISTCHURCH

Dear Darryl,

This letter is to follow up our telephone conversation earlier today.

My colleague, Judy Moore, and I will meet with you at the Papanui office of Child, Youth and Family, 7 Winston Avenue, Christchurch at **2.00pm on Thursday 10 June 2010.**

I will arrange for a taxi chit to be sent you in a separate envelope so that you can get to the meeting.

The purpose of the meeting is to give you the opportunity to talk with us about the concerns you have about your time in care and what your expectations of the Ministry are.

You are welcome to bring a support person to the meeting with you.

If you have any concerns in the meantime can you please contact me on the toll free number: 0508 326459.

Should you need to contact me on the day of the meeting my mobile phone number is 029 3564474.

I look forward to meeting you.

Yours sincerely,

Fiona Wilson
Senior Social Work Advisor
Care, Claims and Resolutions

MINISTRY OF SOCIAL DEVELOPMENT
Te Manatū Whakahiato Ora

National Office, Bowen State Building, Bowen Street, PO Box 1556, Wellington 6140 • Facsimile: 0-4-918 0099

23 July 2010

Darryl Smith
56 Worcester Boulevard
Christchurch 8013

Dear Darryl

This letter is to confirm our conversation yesterday when I told you that I will be
undertaking the review of your case. As I mentioned it may be a couple of months
before I am able to start work on reviewing all the files but I will write to you again
and let you know when I have actually started work.

We are all very pleased to hear that you have now moved into your new flat and we
are pleased we could assist you to do this.

It may be some months before I complete my enquiries but you are welcome to
contact me through the toll free number, 0508 326459 if you have any queries in the
meantime.

Kind regards

Judy Moore
Senior Social Work Advisor MNZASW
Care, Claims and Resolutions Team

MINISTRY OF SOCIAL DEVELOPMENT
Te Manatū Whakahiato Ora

Ministry of Social Development, Bowen State Building, Bowen Street, Wellington 6011, PO Box 1556, Wellington 6140 • Facsimile: 04-916 1100

21 June 2010

Darryl Smith
c/- Alpine View Holiday Park
650 Main South Road
Templeton
CHRISTCHURCH

Dear Darryl,

This letter is to follow up our telephone conversation earlier today.

I'm glad that you felt better after talking with me.

Please find enclosed an envelope which you can send back to our office with the letters you mentioned on the phone. I will arrange to have these copied and will return them to you.

Yours sincerely,

Fiona Wilson
Senior Social Work Advisor
Care, Claims and Resolutions

STATE & CHURCH CARE ABUSE IN 1971 TO 1978

not seen my medical files from Christchurch Hospital so I cannot commit on this.

11. The memories I have of my father at this time are of his abusive physical behaviour towards me. As I had not progressed like the rest of the kids, he found it profoundly irritating and upsetting that I did not speak properly.

12. It is true to say that the greatest support I had was from my grandmother. My memories of her are of total support and caring.

13. I understand that I was first seen, due to developmental problems, by the Christchurch Psychological Services at the Health Clinic in 1969 at the age of 5 years. There is no record on my file of this visit.

MARYLANDS SCHOOL

14. Although there are no other records on my file, in 1971, I spent some time at Marylands School run by the Brothers of St John of God, a Roman Catholic religious order. I was withdrawn from the school due to financial difficulties in the family home. My Father was, at the time, working as a taxi driver, and I seem to recollect that there was a big mortgage on the family home, so money was very tight. I think that my mother was working at the biscuit factory to supplement the family income.

15. Whilst I was at Marylands, I was sexually abused by Brother Keane and Brother Moloney, staff members and older boys. Grant Cameron, a lawyer, is dealing with this matter so it is not included in this statement. All I would add is that no-one knew about the abuse at Marylands at that time.

16. I was admitted to the Riccarton Junior Special Class in February 1973. On 24th February 1973, a medical examination for education placement was undertaken. This examination recorded my antenatal history which stated that, after a threatened miscarriage, I was surgically induced. It was also noted that, as a baby, I had a swollen tongue and ate no solids until after I was a year old. This report also mentioned that at the age of 2-3 years, I had an accident which affected my nose and I had nasal blockage from a crooked septum.

17. I first came to the attention of Social Welfare after somebody made a complaint that they had seen a small child wondering around Riccarton Road at 8pm at night on 14th February 1973. Apparently I supplied my address and phone number and my mother was rung. My mother's response apparently was "oh don't worry, just send him home in a taxi... he's always doing this – he is slightly mental". Based on this report, Social Welfare decided to take a closer look at the home environment.

18. As the family then moved to Nelson, no contact was made with Social Welfare until 5 November 1973. My parents told Social Welfare that I was a problem with a History of absconding, truancy and theft. Apparently I had come to police notice when living in Christchurch.

19. My memories of my early schooling are very negative. I was the object of a lot of ridicule and persecution by other kids. My response to this to run away and steal things. I think I started stealing things because that made me feel good and forget about all the bad things that happened to me. In fact I realize now that this behaviour has followed me right through my life.

20. I don't know when it started, but at least by the age of 8, I was prescribed drugs to help control me and to help calm me down, but I do not know what they were. The medication was introduced during the period that I was at Marylands. I have been told that one of the reasons why the family moved to Nelson was because I was stealing from everybody, including friends of my parents. I think things must have been quite difficult for them, and they probably resented me because of it.

21. When I was 10 years old, I remember going on a Holiday to Tahuna Beach. I was sexually assaulted and raped. This was by somebody that I did not know and I have never seen since. I remember thinking that I couldn't tell my father because he was drinking so much and then he wouldn't have believed me and I would have got a hiding for lying. This event, I think, made my behaviour considerably worse and my parents found it impossible to keep me under any kind of adequate surveillance or supervision.

22. This event occurred on or around 4 November 1973, and the fact that we were at Tahuna Motor Camp is noted on my file. Within 2 days, I was found at Nelson Airport trying to get a flight to Wellington. I had stolen money to buy the ticket. After this event, my running off and often stealing, because a pattern of behaviour.

23. At this time, admission to Campbell Park School was discussed but they had no room. I see from my file that I was also on a waiting list for Templeton Hospital. I spent some time in Templeton because my admission to Campbell Park was delayed and I guess it was felt that it would give my parents a break.

TEMPLETON HOSPITAL

24. First time I went there was before my mother had my sister Rochelle, born on the 8th of March 1973 and why I was there I was going to Riccarton Primary School.

25. I actually had 2 admissions to Templeton Hospital, but I have been unable to access those files as I was advised that the files were destroyed in 1999. I want to record in this statement what happened to me on my first admission, exactly what date I went there, I do not know but it was certainly just prior to Christmas 1973. I was 10 years old at the time. I know this because it was referred to in my Social Welfare files.

SEXUAL ABUSE

32. On 1 April 1974, the same day I was taken under warrant, I was sent to a Family Home which was run by a Mrs Alice Strawbridge in Tahuna in Nelson. I remember that I was only there for a few days as she was quite physically abusive. I was really wound up and I was told that I was going to be sent to Christchurch quite soon and I recollect Mrs Strawbridge telling me that if I didn't go to sleep, I would get a hiding, I couldn't sleep of course and that was exactly what happened. I got a hiding.

33. A few days later I was transferred to another Family Home run by a Mrs Barrie in Moray Avenue in Christchurch. By this time I had started wetting the bed. I know this because Mrs Barrie rang Social Welfare and asked for many more pairs of pyjamas for me. I was not there long, but Mrs Barrie was physically abusive towards me. By her hitting me a lot. Making no marks on my face so social welfare couldn't see the marks. But only on the body.

34. I remember that I absconded from Mrs Barrie's home at some stage, and everybody thought that I had gone to find my grandmother. The Family Home was very overcrowded. It stated in my file that only 24 boys were supposed to be there, but in fact there were over 30. After spending time with an aunt over Easter 1974, I returned to the Family Home and was greeted by Mrs Barrie which was observed by Social Welfare.

35. Mrs Barrie was described in a report dated 1 May 1974 as being verbally aggressive which was at the time thought to be "inappropriate". If Social Welfare were concern about Mrs Barrie's ability to care for me, or any other children in her care, I do not understand why they left me there.

CAMPBELL PARK SCHOOL

36. I was finally admitted to Campbell Park on the 29 May 1974. A report from Campbell Park School dated 30 May 1974 listed their impressions of me at this time. I was described as an untidy, pathetic child, a loner, selfish, with a good imagination. This report also stated that I had been subjected to bullying from other boys.

37. From the time I arrived at Campbell Park until I left, I was subjected to sexual and physical abuse by both older boys in the house and staff members.

SEXUAL ABUSE

38. Every new boy that arrived at Campbell park was subject to an initiation ceremony. This was undertaken by the older boys at the school and happened to all the new boys. Every boy was blanketed, by that I mean held down with a blanket over your body, and then raped. As a new boy, you learnt very quickly not to fight back. Like others, I just gave up.

39. In this statement I want to name the abusers and what they did to me. I know that Campbell Park was run by the Ministry of Education but it

was Social Welfare who placed me there, and I hold them responsible for what happened to me.

40. The school was divided into houses and each house had its own housemaster. The overall principal of the school while I was there was Mr Aspden, so I shall start with him. Mr Aspden used to get the staff to bring me to his office because he wanted to talk to me. This, in fact, was not true. In the privacy of his office, he was sexually abusive; he would touch me and kiss me, and play with my penis. Other incidents that occurred happened in the gym and sometimes in the swimming pool changing sheds. Out of sight, Mr Aspden would continue to touch, kiss and fondle my genital area.

41. I was put in Taylor House, and I recollect a number of teachers who sexually abused me also. The first was Mr Shakespeare, who would come into my dormitory and take me to the toilets outside. He would play with my genitals and anus. He would then rape me by penetrating me with his penis. He would often insist that we went on walks around the property, I realize now that this was so that no-one could see what was happening. First time Mr Shakespeare abused me was at Campbell Park and then Mr Shakespeare left working at Campbell Park to work in Christchurch at Stanmore Road Boys Home.

42. One day I remember Mr Shakespeare dropped me off at my grandmother's place. It was then that he realized who I was. "And second time he abused me was at Stanmore Road Boys Home in Christchurch before he meet my grandmother." It was only after that the sexual abuse stop from him. I also found out years later that he had in fact been a friend of my mother.

43. I remember that the same year, I had another teacher, a Mr Holt. He also liked preying on young boys and at every opportunity he would isolate me, play with my genitals and anally penetrate me. This happened on a regular basis with Mr Holt until he left the school. I do not know what date that was.

44. There was a woman at Campbell Park School, a Miss Savage, I admit that I found her interesting, not that she was beautiful. I mean as boys we would fantasise about sex with a beautiful woman. Miss Miss Savage liked young boys. I remember once she took me to her room and asked me to take of my pants. She then gave me oral sex and asked her to get in bed with her, so I did. When she asked me to have sex with her, I did.

45. The matron of Campbell Park School was a Mrs Campbell, an older woman. I think she started there in about 1975. This only happened the one time, but she would fondle my genitals, tell me that I was a big boy and that she liked me. I seem to remember that she was quite old, or that was how she seemed to me at the time. I imagine that she is dead now. Years later I heard a rumour that, in fact she had died because she had been pushed down some stairs. I have no idea if this was true.

46. After Mr Holt left, I recollect another teacher by the name of Mrs Johnson. I remember that Mrs Johnson was my teacher in 1976. She was

the one who used to send me to Mr O'Connor for punishment if I played up in her class. I guess Mrs Johnson liked young boys, just like her husband. I think I was 12 years old at the time and I did not want this woman to come on to me. She asked me to have sex with her which made me sick. Sometimes she would take me to her house in the village and make me have sex with her there.

47.   Mrs Johnson's husband was also abusive to me. I remember this well because it started when I had to go to Dunedin Hospital for an operation on my nose. I do know that I was admitted to Dunedin Hospital on 7 November 1974. I recollect that I spent my birthday in hospital. The staff were very kind to me. I was discharged from Hospital on 12 November 1974, and I was put in the care of Mr & Mrs Johnson who would take me to their home and give me dinner. Everything was fine until Mr Johnson would take me in his car back to Campbell Park. I remember that he took me to a shed on the school property and raped me. I do not know if he was directly employed by Campbell Park but he was certainly there a lot. I remember that he abused me in the dormitory at night or in the day time if I was sick in bed. Just being there meant that you were something to be used. Mr Johnson was a very cruel man. I remember that when I heard that he had been killed in a boat accident at Lake Benmore, I was very happy when this happened.

48.   Principal at the school, a Mr Willis, also liked abusing young boys. I remember he had his own office and would take me in there to talk about my spelling and reading. This used to happen about once a week. After he had finished talking about my spelling and reading, he would then make me do sexual things to him. He would then make me pull down my pants and play with my penis and make me lean over his desk so that he could anally penetrate me.

49.   There was also a man by the name of Pat Welsh. At some time, I think he was housemaster of Campbell Park School, that is what I remember anyway. He was a very big man. He also liked young boys. He used to take me to "The Cave" and get me to kiss him on the lips and make me say that I loved him. After I had said that, he would remove my pants and anally rape me. Mr Bernie Welsh, I think he was second in charge at Campbell Park School at some time. He had a favourite location, "the castle" where he would sexually abuse me. This was very regular event.

50.   Mr O'Connor was the last teacher I had at Campbell Park School. I think that was somewhere between 1977 to 1978. I remember him because he had an American left-hand driver motor home. I think that all the boys thought this was pretty exciting but the motor home was used as a private place to abuse. He would always say to me "I will make you do as you are told one way or another". Mr O'Connor would perform oral sex on me and then make me do the same to him. He used to get me on his bed in the motor home and then anally rape me.

51.   Mr Medcalf was a housemaster. He used to take boys to his home and abuse them if he could. Another favourite place of his was the gym and

sometimes the dorm. I was sexually abused by him on a number of occasions. I do remember his wife, she was always very kind to me. She didn't know what was going on. Mr Medcalf would rape me and kiss me. Raping me in anally.

52.   Another of the female staff was Mrs Joan Gibbons. Like Mrs Johnson, she liked young boys and forced me to have sex with her.

53.   Mr Mateos, I think that was his name, also abused me. I think I was in the Disney House at the time. I remember this because I had my leg in a bandage but I cannot remember why. He would come on to me and start fondling my genital area. He was a very fat man, who would never walk anywhere because he was so lazy. He used to drive everywhere and would make me get into his car so that he could take me to the dining room. That way he could get boys alone. Sometimes at night, I remember, he would get me in the TV room, I don't know where the other boys were, but he would take my pyjama pants off and perform oral sex. Another favourite of his was the outside toilets.

54.   One of my housemasters at sometime, I'm not sure what year it was, was a Mr Parsons. He was also an abuser. His story was a little bit different as what he wanted to do was to teach me survival in the bush. I seem to remember that he was in the medical unit with the army in Oamaru. He would take me into the bush on the pretext of teaching me, and then ask me to perform oral sex on him. He would then do it to me.

55.   I think it was in 1978 that I was abused by Stuart Ellwood. I think it was him. I know that I was only one of the many boys. I remember being in my dormitory asleep one night when I was awoken with somebody playing with my genital area. It was him. He would then take me to the outside toilets and tell me to take off my pyjamas. He would then kiss me and run his hands over my body. I remember that he then got on his knees to give me a blow job and buttocks and push his fingers into my anus. He would then anally rape me.

LOCATIONS

56.   A favourite place for all the sexual abusers was "the cave". I used to call it the cave of hell. That's my name for it because of what happened there. It was a favourite place for the older boys and for staff. The older boys used to take the weaker and younger boys with them to the cave so that they could sexually or physically abused them there. This happened to me on a regular basis.

57.   Another favourite place was the graveyard which was on a hill behind Campbell Park School. Older boys used this place to sexually abuse younger boys as did the staff. I spent quite a lot of time being abused by them. It was probably a good spot because it was out of sight. An area that was out of bounds was the flying fox area. I do not think it was checked. This place was favoured by the boys, not the staff. All the boys went there to have fights or to rape the younger or weaker boys. Physical

size and strength gave the older boys all the power. It didn't help that I was small for my age.

58. Another favourite place for the opportunity to abuse was the swimming pool and changing rooms. I remember they were "no go" zones in winter time. I don't think there was ever a teacher supervising what happened in the changing rooms. I remember in summer when we would go up for a swim, the teachers would go to the pool and leave the boys to change into swim wear. This meant that there was the opportunity for boys to be sexually abused. I was one of them.

59. The gym was okay but everybody knew it was a place where older boys would bully or sexually abuse younger boys, just like in the cave. They would make us do anything they wanted us to do. Sexual abuse did happened in the gym. I remember an incident that happened not long after swimming with another older boy called Steve Cross. He forced me to perform oral sex on him. He also forced me to fondle him and then he raped me. I heard years later that he went to court for sexual abuse of young children. I think that he had lots of victims.

PHYSICAL ABUSE:

60. Physical abuse occurred on a daily basis. Almost all the teachers or staff who sexually abused, also physically abused. The most common form of physical abuse was the use of fists and hitting to my body. The following teachers who did this, it was so frequent I cannot give dates, were Mrs Johnson, Mr Barrie Welsh, Mr Pat Welsh, Mrs Joan Gibbons and Mr Mattocs. Mr O'Connor also physically abuse me, usually saying to me "this will make a man out of you". Mr Wering used to take great pleasure in thinking up new ways of punishing boys. One of his favourites was making me carry bricks up and down the hill behind the house until I was exhausted. My memory of him is that he was very cruel.

61. Kevin Froggatt, like me, was also physically abused on a regular basis by Mr O'Connor and other staff members.

VERBAL ABUSE:

62. I guess when you get told are a nuisance or a bloody pest every hour of the day, you get to believe it. Some things stick in my mind. For example, I remember Mrs Gibbons withholding my pudding one lunch time, telling me that I was too fat. Mr Mattocs, the house master who was so lazy he would just drive everywhere, was always telling me that I was useless at everything. There are too many incidents for me to list here, all I can say is that verbal abuse was part of every day life at Campbell Park.

OLDER BOYS:

63. There was another boy at Campbell Park School that I knew. His name was Kevin Frogott. I remember that he was sexually abused by Mrs Savage.

64. Another boy I remember was Barry Alan Ryder. Who was in Taylor House when I was in Disney House. He was sexually abused on a regular basis by both older boys and staff members. I also remember Barry Ryder being sexually abused by Stuart Ellwood in the garden area of the school. I remember seeing Barry being sexually abused by bigger boys and by the staff member. He was a very small boy and so everyone used called him "spider Ryder" because of his size. He would often be dragged down to the trees and then raped. The staff always used to tell us that we were being watched. That is absolute rubbish .

65. One of the worst abusers, in terms of older boys, was a boy that I remember was called Jason Q. He was in Taylor House, the same house that I was in for a quite some time. I would be lying in my bed and he would just come in. He used to tell me that if I didn't give him a blow job, and let him penetrate me, he would give me a severe beating. Jason would also make sexual advances in the TV room. Not only did he fondle me, but he also fondled another boy called Richard Evans. I saw him being abused by Jason Q.

66. Another one of the older boys was Christopher Truscott. He also used to sexually abuse and hurt younger boys.

67. I remember a particular time when we were being sent by bus to Lyttleton. We were going to catch the Ferry Rangatira between Lyttleton and Wellington. I have no recollection where the staff were, but we would all team up, the older boys all together and the younger boys separately. The older boys would always take any opportunity, when they knew that there was no staff around, to abuse the younger boys on the ferry. This happened to me twice that I recollect but I do not know the exact dates.

68. It was common for us boys to move around unescorted. For example, I flew home to my parents' house for a school break in the August 1974 school holidays. It started on the vacation schedule that I was allowed to travel unescorted. My parents were supposed to pick me up at the airport but were unable to.

69. I spent my first year at Campbell Park School in Taylor House. I had an assessment on 26 February 1975 with the Psychological Services of the Department of Education. I was reported as making progress and that I was keen to learn to read. I had improved with my vocabulary and comprehension. An earlier report by Campbell Park suggested that I had great difficulty finding social acceptance. I was easily distressed, and tended to prefer to be alone. Only part of this report is on my file so I do not know what date it was undertaken.

70. My parents moved from Jenna Road in Nelson out to a rural area in Belgrove, Wakefield in late August 1975. I had continued to travel home (unescorted) during the school holidays. My parents, based on the Social Welfare files seemed happy with my progress. So much so, that it was

thought that I may be discharged from Campbell Park at the end of 1976 so that I could live at home and attend Waimea Intermediate School in Richmond starting in 1977.

71. I can see from my files that the decision as to whether or not I should return home, and attend a local school was a matter of debate. My behaviour was reported on a week by week basis starting in term one of 1976. It did cover the whole year but it seems that this report showed that I was not liked, either by the staff or other boys. This report also mentioned that older boys bullied me to keep me in line. I was referred to frequently in very negative ways. I was described as a pest, a perpetual nuisance, constantly whining, constantly in trouble with other boys because of my own actions, and noisy.

72. Other comments in this report, for example from 8 June 1976 for the next few weeks, referred to my being bullied, teased and thumped by older boys. There was nothing in this report that told me that any of the teachers did anything to intervene. Most of the time, it seemed like they just thought I was not discharged home and stayed on at Campbell Park until the end of 1976.

73. My relationship with my parents started to deteriorate in early 1977, not long after going home. On 23 March 1977, I was placed temporarily in a Family Home because I had started absconding from school. This was the Tahunanui Family Home in Great Street in Nelson, and was run by a Mrs Janice Health. My records refer to a "breakdown of family home in Nelson" after my difficult behaviour. In one instance, I tried to burn a relation's shed down. Social Welfare was of the opinion that I had returned home too early. I remained at the Tahunanui Family Home for only 2 weeks whilst an application was made to have me readmitted to Campbell Park.

74. While I was in the care of Mr & Mrs Health at the Tahunanui Family Home, I was physically and sexually abused by Mr Health. I was at the Family Home longer then 2 weeks, I think three months. Mr Health would make me do oral sex on him. Mr Health rape me anally.

75. I was transferred to the Boys Home in Stanmore Road in Christchurch on 6 April 1977. The remarks on the transfer note that I have located on my file state that, not only had I absconded, but in fact had committed burglaries. I don't know how long I was at Stanmore Road Boy's Home before I was admitted back to Campbell Park. I don't think it was very long, but I can find no transfer documentation on my records. I do know that it was prior to August 1977, as I resumed my visits to my family home in the August school holidays. I was raped and beaten up a lot when I was staying at Stanmore Road Boys' Home from 1974-78 on or between my school holidays .

76. In October 1977, my parents decided to move to Australia. They had not planned to take me, believing that I needed to finish my schooling at Campbell Park. This meant that an alternative holiday placement needed

to be found. Nothing long term could be found, so I was transferred back to the Boy's Home for Christmas.

77.   On 16 February 1978, a reassessment by Psychological services was undertaken. I was at the time 14 years and 3 months old. The report stated that I continued to make progress over the previous 12 months, particularly with reading. Relationships with other students and the staff remained the same as per the report referred to earlier in 1976. By that I mean that I continued to irritate staff and fellow pupils. The overall recommendation was that I be discharged from Campbell Park at the end of 1978 and sent to live with my parents, who were at that time living in Queensland.

78.   There is not a great deal on my file for 1978. There was a progress report dated 29 May 1978, which stated that I was receiving little mail from my parents. There was a slight improvement in social attitudes which was thought to be due to the controlled environment that I was living in.

79.   In a report dated 9 October 1976 written by a Mr Willis, the principal at the school, commented that I had been involved in some form of sexual misconduct. He stated; "It may have been only mutual masturbation but the fact that he has been involved with an older, known molester of little girls and boys, bears commenting upon. While only one recent incident has been recorded, there is a general attitude amongst the boys that would suggest that the problem is greater than what appears on the surface." I was never told about the matter of the older boy was a sex offender.

80.   This is the first time any comment was placed on my file regarding sexual misconduct. I am not sure who Mr Willis was referring to. What was obvious was the fact that Mr Willis (an abuser himself) tried to play down what was really going on at Campbell Park. There is no reference to an inquiry, any talks to the boys, or any form of counseling. If there had been misconduct by someone that was known to the school, I would have thought they would spring into action, but when I think of my experiences there, that would be too much to expect.

81.   In November 1978, Social Welfare wrote to Children's Services in Brisbane asking that they organize a Child Care Officer to visit my parents prior to my returning to them in Australia. I was discharged from Campbell Park on 14 December 1978 and discharged from the care of Social Welfare on 4 January 1979.

82.   On 18 April 1979, I was picked up in Christchurch by the police. I had actually returned to Auckland from Brisbane on 16 April 1979 and then flown to Christchurch. When I was picked up the police, I was hungry and was described as being in a dirty and unkempt condition. I was admitted to the Boy's Home by the police on a complaint of "not under proper control". I appeared in court in April 1979 for stealing a bicycle and was returned to Australia, I believe, on 4 May 1979.

83.   When I was in Australia, I was mugged and raped by 4 men. They put a knife to my throat and one had a gun. This happened near a railway

to care for me. It wasn't just once, it happened over years in different places. Prison was a safer place to be at the time. But why there suffered abuse there too. From rape to beatings from other inmates.

MR.P.R.PARSONS
HOUSEMASTER

Mr Parsons was my housemaster and wanted to teach me survival in the bush.

The survival he wanted to teach me wasn't the survival in the bush. He was in the Medical Unit with the Army in Oamaru the time.

He would take me into the bushs to make me do oral sex on him and he would then do it on me and sometimes he would do oral sex on me and then rape me.

P.G.ASPDEN
PRINCIPAL OF CAMPBELL PARK

Mr Aspden would take me to the gym and sometimes to the swimming pool changing sheds and sexually abuse me there.

He would do alot of touching & kissing, feeling my penis area.

He would call me to his office and would say to the staff that he wanted to talk to me in his office to look at the stamp collection (books) my parents left in my care to look after into I fly to Australia in 1978. My parents left for Australia in 1977 leaving me at Campbell Park School of horror and hell.

But this wasn't true.
He got me into his office to touch me and kiss me and play with my penis and if anyone walk into the office he had the stamp albums out of the safe and opened and with a stamp price book.

THE CAVE OF HELL

The older Boys from Campbell House would go to Disney House and pick the weaker and younger boys to go with them to the Cave.

The Cave of Hell is my nickname for the place because of want happened there.

The older boys would then take me and some of the other boys to the cave and sexually and physically abuse me and the others there.

And sometimes in the Scrum and jam rape has there.

But the Campbell House boys that were doing this would take there turns with each boy into each of has had been rape by all of the gang.

BRUCE HOLT
1974-1976
Class Teacher

Mr Holt would get me in the classroom by myself and would first of all make me do oral sex on him and then he would do it on me.

And then he would get me over a desk and rape me.

STANMORE BOYS HOME
FROM 1974-1979

In 1974 I was but on a plane at Nelson Airport and staying the night at the family Home in Tahunanui, Nelson for the night by the order of the court for not being in proper control from 1/4/74 to 2/4/74 I was in there care and I still get the nightmares from the physical abuse that happened that night from Alice Strawbridge, the address was 71 Green Street, Tahunanui, Nelson and that is were the family home was at the time. My mother saw my off at the airport.

At the Boys home there was alot of older boys sexually and physically abusing the younger boys when they first night at the boys home the older boys would sexually abuse by raping you and then physically abusing you after they rape you. I got that alot because I was only 10 years old at the time and from there I went to Mrs M.M. Barry at 76 Moorny Ave, Christchurch 5/8/74 were I was physically abused by the older children.

That is why I ran away from the Family home run by Miss M.M. Barry she would let the older children hit me and at night was not safe because an older boy who was living there would come into my room and rape me and told me if I tell anyone he would kill me.

J.Kean, Manager, Stanmore Road Boys Home physically abused me on the 3/6/74 in the office.

Mr Brandon Physical abused me why in his care on a day outing.

STEVE CROSS
SEXUALLY ABUSED ME

When I was at Stanmore Road Boys Home when I was on my school holidays from Campbell Park School I was having a swim in the pool and Steve come into the pool and got his hands on to my penis and started playing with it and then kiss me on the lips and after I got out of the swimming pool he followed me to the gym where I was having a shower and he got into the shower with me and rape me.

He use to get me when I was in the garden and he would make me do oral sex on him.

MR WOOD
SUPERINTENT

Mr Wood use to have the office in the front of the Boys Home and he would get boys to come into his office and he would do oral sex on them and then make them do oral sex on him.

In one chance I was in his office and he got my pants down and rape me and then made me do oral sex on him.

MRS FRASER
With glasses and with brown - blonde hair & fat
PHYSICAL ABUSE

When I was in her care and played up all the time because I hated her very much for the cruel things she use to do with me.

She use to make me go with her to the garden at the back of the boys home and get me to do oral sex on older boys why she watch and then she would hit me for doing it.

MR BRANDEN - 1979

By making me do oral sex on him and he would rape me by fucking me.

He would do this every night and I hated him for that.

That stop when he moved to Disney House.

When we would go on the holidays first by bus and then by overnight ship. Some of the older boys would rape me in my cabin or the cabin room and the boy that was older was at Campbell House and I was in Taylor and he would take me to his cabin sometimes or keep me in my cabin and he and other boys from Campbell House would sexually abuse me and other boys from my house when were on the ship at night.

This happen alot. Into Campbell Park School stop putting his kids on the ferry and then by plane and then that stop.

Campbell Park School was under the Ministry of Education because it was a school so they employed the staff that sexually abused me so they are at felt.

The Department of Social Welfare back in 1975 Who sent me to that school put me at risk of being sexually abuse by staff and boys.

The Department of Social Welfare today is Child, Youth & Family.

I was peer pressured into having sex with older boys.

MR. O'CONNOR
Teacher

Mr O'Connor was my last teacher at Campbell Park School in 1977-1978.

Mr O'Connor would give my cruelb punishment if I got in trouble in Mrs Johnson class room back in 1976 with hitting me alot with his fits were it didn't show.

He would say this will make you a man.

One time he would take me on a trip in his American left hand drive motor home and he would drive to the school with it and had alot of classic vehicles and would being them to the school. In the motor home he would rape me in it.

Mr O'Connor was my school teacher at Campbell Park School a longtime.

When he was sexually abusing me he would do oral sex on me and then make do peal sex on me and would rape me by getting me on his bed in the motor home and would fuck the ass off me.

He said to me I will make you do this you are my property.

MR. MEDCALF

A housemaster would take me to his house when there was noone there and would sexually abuse me and also get me in the gym and sometimes in the dormitory...

But his wife was always very kind to me and always remembered my birthday.

Me and Kevin Froggatt were also physically abused by Mr Medcalf.

CHILD YOUTH & FAMILY LETTERS OVER THE ABUSE

7 April 2004

Darryl W Smith
Private Bag 3000
WANGANUI

Dear Mr Smith

I refer to you letter to Ms Maplesden of our office dated 31 March 2004. Ms Maplesden is no longer working in our National Office and accordingly I am responding to your letter.

A claim against the Department of Child, Youth and Family must contain sufficient information for the Department to be able to clearly understand in what way you believe the Department has acted inappropriately and must clearly set out the evidence you have in support of any allegations you wish to make.

A claim also requires evidence of harm you alleged was caused to you by the actions of the Department. Expert psychiatric evidence is required in order to support a claim. I have received your letter of 7 April. The psychologist's report appears to be missing some pages. You may wish to forward a full copy to me.

I advise that you seek legal advice to assist you with the making of a claim against the Department. You may be entitled to legal aid to assist you in the preparation of such a claim.

Yours faithfully

Zoe Griffith
Acting Chief Legal Officer

Legal Services
Level 1, Charles Fergusson
West Block
PO Box 3443,
Wellington, NZ
Phone: 04 916 9122
Fax: 04 916 9195

18 December 2002

Darryl Smith
26 Bowenmouth Crescent
CHRISTCHURCH

Dear Darryl Smith

Thank you for your letter of 22 November 2002 regarding the time you spent in the care of the Department of Social Welfare in the 1970s, and your complaint that you were sexually abused during this period by staff in the family home and boys' home you were placed in.

Regrettably, I am unable to comment further on the issues you raised until I have had a chance to look at the information contained on your personal file, and it is not possible for me to do that until I receive clarification of your date of birth from you. This information is required to ensure that the correct files are retrieved when searching for your records in the Department's archives.

Could you please write back to me with this information so I can address the original issues you have raised, or, if you would prefer, you can call me directly on 09 918 9254.

Yours sincerely

Garth Young
Manager, Ministerials Unit

National Office
Level 1, Bowen State Building
Bowen St, PO Box 2620
Wellington, NZ
Phone: 04 918 9100
Phone: 0508 Family
or 0808 326 459
Fax 04 918 9089

Department of Child, Youth and Family Services - Te Iwi Awhina i te Tamaiti, te Rangatahi, me ona o te Whānau

child
youth
family

7 January 2003

Darryl W Smith
C/- Christchurch Prison
Private Bag 4726
CHRISTCHURCH

Dear Darryl

The Chief Executive of Child, Youth and Family, Jackie Pivac, has asked me to thank you for your letters, dated 19 and 20 December 2002, regarding allegations of abuse.

It has been referred to the Department's legal team for response and they will contact you in due course.

Yours sincerely

Garth Young
Manager, Ministerials Unit

Chief Executive's Office
Bowen State Building
Bowen St, PO Box 2620
Wellington, NZ
Phone: 04 918 9110
Phone: 0508 Family
or 0508 326 459
Fax: 04 916 9281

Department of Child, Youth and Family Services - Te Tari Āwhina i te Tamaiti, te Rangatahi, tae atu ki te Whānau
www.cyf.govt.nz

child,
youth
and
family

7 January 2003

Darryl Smith
Private Bag 4726
Templeton
CHRISTCHURCH

Dear Darryl Smith

I wrote to you in the middle of December 2002 seeking further information from you to enable me to respond to your letter of 22 November 2002. It appears, from the subsequent correspondence recently received from you, that you may not have received this letter and so I have enclosed a further copy for your information. I would appreciate it if you could contact me, either by mail or phone, with the information requested, so the original issues you raised can be addressed.

With regard to your most recent letters, I understand that these will be addressed by a member of the Department's legal staff in due course.

Yours sincerely

Garth Young
Manager, Ministerials Unit

National Office
Level 5, Bowen State Building
Bowen St, PO Box 2620
Wellington, NZ
Phone: 04 918 9100
Phone: 0508 Family
or 0508 326 459
Fax: 04 918 9299

Department of Child, Youth and Family Services • Te Tari Āwhina i te Tamaiti, te Rangatahi, tae atu ki te Whānau

9 January 2003

Daryl W Smith
Private Bag 4726
Templeton
CHRISTCHURCH

child,
youth
and
family

Dear Mr Smith

Re: Your letter of Complaint

Your letter of complaint with allegations of the sexual abuse you suffered while in the Stanmore Road Boys Home has been referred to me.

Your letter does not provide sufficient information to allow the Department to conduct an investigation and to assess whether the claims that you make are such that compensation is properly payable to you. The investigations of historical allegations of the nature that you have made are often difficult and dependent on the location of files and witnesses. It has been the experience of the Department that the investigation of such claims is assisted by the preparation of a draft statement of claim which allows a focused investigation. As a result the Department now requires a draft statement of claim prior to initiating an investigation.

The statement of claim is a document that sets out clearly all of the allegations that you wish to make in detail together with any names of those you are making allegations against. If you are alleging that you have suffered harm then the detail of that harm should also be clearly set out. If you are claiming mental injury as a result of what has occurred to you the Department will also seek evidence of that by way of any psychiatric or psychological reports that you may have. You may wish to seek legal advice on the preparation of this document.

Once the draft statement of claim has been received I will investigate your claim on behalf of the Department and will make contact with you with regard to the Department's response.

Yours sincerely,

Zoe Griffiths
Solicitor

Legal Service
Level 4, Charles Fergusson
West Block
PO Box 2620,
Wellington, NZ
Phone: 04 918 9122
Fax 04 918 9291

Department of Child, Youth and Family Services - Te Tari Āwhina i te Tamaiti, te Rangatahi, me ona iti te Whānau
f_zeroad0901035.doc

13 January 2003

Darryl Smith
Private Bag 4726
Templeton
CHRISTCHURCH

Dear Darryl Smith

Thank you for your letter of 22 November 2002 regarding your time spent in care under the then Department of Social Welfare, in which you have stated that you were sexually abused by staff and other children in care at a family home in Nelson and the Stanmore Road Boys Home. I have also just received your letter of 3 January 2003, in which you state that there is nothing in your file to confirm your previous statement, as you had never told anyone what had happened.

Having retrieved your files from archive storage and perused them for information relating to your claim, I can confirm that there is nothing on file to indicate that any sexual abuse took place at the family home in Nelson or the Stanmore Road Boys Home. Without further detailed information about names, places, dates, people you may have told, etc., it would be very difficult to provide you with a suitable reply in respect of this.

Should you wish to take this matter further, you will need to provide a Statement of Claim to the Department, which can then be considered by members of the legal staff here in National Office. I would suggest that you obtain the services of a solicitor to assist you in compiling such a claim, as the information contained within it needs to be very specific.

I am aware that you have written about this matter subsequent to your 22 November letter, and that the suggestion that you lodge a Statement of Claim has already been made. I fully endorse this suggestion.

I regret that I was not able to provide you with a more positive response in this instance.

Yours sincerely

Shannon Pakura
Acting Chief Executive

Department of Child, Youth and Family Services • Te Tari Awhina i te Tamaiti, te Rangatahi, me etu hi te Whanau
www.cyf.govt.nz

Chief Executive's Office
Bowen State Building
Bowen St, PO Box 2620
Wellington, NZ
Phone: 04 918 9110
Phone: 0508 Family
or 0808 326 459
Fax: 04 918 9091

POLICE LETTERS OF THE HISTORIAL ABUSE

New Zealand
POLICE

13 February 2003

Mr D W Smith
Private Bag 4728
Fendalton
CHRISTCHURCH

Dear Mr Smith

I am writing to advise you that I have received the letter you forwarded to the Minister of Police regarding allegations of abuse during the period 1973 to 1976.

I intend have enquiries completed to identify whether a complaint has been made regarding these allegations. On receipt of that information I will write to you again.

Yours sincerely

Detective Superintendent M Burgess
Acting District Commander
Canterbury

Safer Communities Together

CANTERBURY DISTRICT HEADQUARTERS
Cnr Hereford Street and Cambridge Terrace, PO Box 2109, Christchurch
Telephone: 0-3-379 3999, Facsimile: 0-5-363 5819

New Zealand
POLICE

WW 52209

Ref:

27 February 2003

Mr Darryl William Smith
C/o Paparua Prison
Private Bag 5726
Templeton
CHRISTCHURCH

Dear Mr Smith

ALLEGATIONS OF HISTORICAL SEXUAL ABUSE

Your letters relating to your desire to make statements regarding complaints of sexual abuse suffered by you have been forwarded to the Hornby CIB (file 030121/5563 refers).

This matter will be directed to a suitably qualified investigator who will arrange to visit the prison and obtain detailed statements from you regarding these incidents.

Due to current workloads and staffing levels, it could be several weeks before you are contacted.

Should there be any change in your circumstances, please advise me immediately.

Yours faithfully

D J Landreth
Detective Senior Sergeant
Hornby

New Zealand
POLICE
Nga Pirihimana O Aotearoa

3 March 2003

Mr Darryl W Smith
Private Bag 4726
Fendalton
CHRISTCHURCH

Dear Sir

On 3 February 2003, you wrote to the Minister of Police, the Honourable George Hawkins. Your letter was referred to the Commissioner of Police who in turn referred it to myself. In your letter you sought compensation and apologies from the Crown regarding alleged child abuse.

I am advised that you have made an initial complaint regarding these events. This initial complaint will be formalised in due course, when a comprehensive statement about these events will be taken from you. Any subsequent Police investigation will be determined by the nature and extent of those allegations.

Until such time as a thorough investigation has been completed, the Minister of Police is unable to address your request.

Yours faithfully

Superintendent S J Manderson
District Commander
Canterbury

Safer Communities Together

NEW ZEALAND POLICE, CANTERBURY DISTRICT HEADQUARTERS
Cnr Hereford Street and Cambridge Terrace, P.O. Box 2109, Christchurch
Telephone: 0-3-379 5999, Facsimile: 0-3-363 5616

CLAIM BY PLAINTIFF

CLAIM BY PLAINTIFF

The plaintiff repeats the allegations contained in paragraphs 1 – 49 inclusive and says –

50. The plaintiff first came to the attention of Social Welfare on 14 February 1973.

51. The plaintiff had two admissions to Templeton Hospital; in March 1973 and December 1973. The plaintiff's December admission was arranged, or approved by, the Director-General or his agents. The plaintiff was just 10 years of age while he was a patient at Templeton Hospital. His legal status at Templeton is unknown.

52. On 1 April 1974, the plaintiff was committed to the care of the Superintendent. The plaintiff remained a state ward until 4 January 1979.

53. On 1 April 1974, the plaintiff was placed with Mrs Alice Strawbridge at the Tahuna Family Home in Nelson.

54. In early April 1974, the plaintiff was placed with Mrs Barrie at the Moray Avenue Family Home in Christchurch, where he resided until 29 May 1974 or thereabouts.

55. On 29 May 1974, the plaintiff was admitted to Campbell Park School. The plaintiff remained at Campbell Park from time to time until 14 December 1978.

56. On 23 March 1977, the plaintiff was placed temporarily in the Tahunanui Family Home, which was operated by Mrs Janice Heath. The plaintiff remained at the Tahunanui Family Home until 6 April 1977.

57. On 6 April 1977, and various other dates between 1974 and 1977 the plaintiff was placed in Stanmore Road, in Christchurch. The date on which the plaintiff left Stanmore Road is unknown, although the plaintiff believes that it was prior to August 1977.

First cause of action in relation to the first defendant – breach of fiduciary duty

58. The Director-General, by his staff and/or agents, further breached the duty referred to in paragraph 13. The plaintiff refers to the particulars below.

Tahuna Family Home: physical assaults

59. On dates he does not now recall, but when he resided at the Tahuna Family Home, the plaintiff was beaten by Mrs Alice Strawbridge, who ran the home, as punishment for not going to sleep. The physical assaults were so severe that the plaintiff sustained a black eye.

Moray Avenue Family Home: physical assaults

60. On dates he does not now recall, but on regular occasions when he resided at the Moray Avenue Family Home, the plaintiff was hit by Mrs Barrie, who ran the Family Home. The beatings caused the plaintiff to suffer bruising on his body and he was unable to sit down or attend school for several days afterwards.

14

Moray Avenue Family Home: inappropriate monitoring

61. On 1 May 1974, Social Welfare staff monitoring the plaintiff's placement, described the caregiver at the Family Home, Mrs Barrie, as verbally aggressive, which the Social Welfare agents found to be inappropriate behaviour. Despite this, the plaintiff remained in the care of Mrs Barrie until 29 May 1974.

Campbell Park: sexual assaults

Sexual assaults by Mr Aspden against the plaintiff

62. On dates that he does not now recall, but on regular occasions while he resided at Campbell Park, the plaintiff was sexually abused by the Principal of Campbell Park School, whose name was Mr Aspden.

    Particulars of abuse

    (a) Mr Aspden arranged for staff members to bring the plaintiff into his office to so that Mr Aspden could "talk" to the plaintiff;

    (b) When the plaintiff arrived at his office, Mr Aspden would inappropriately touch and kiss the plaintiff, and play with the plaintiff's penis;

    (c) The abuse referred to in subparagraph (b) above also took place in the gym, the swimming pool and the changing sheds.

Sexual abuse by Mr Shakespeare against the plaintiff

63. On dates that he does not now recall, but while he resided at Campbell Park's Taylor House, the plaintiff was sexually abused by a male staff member named Mr Shakespeare.

    Particulars of abuse

    (a) On regular occasions, Mr Shakespeare would come into the plaintiff's dormitory and take the plaintiff to the toilets outside;

(b) There, Mr Shakespeare would play with the plaintiff's genitals and digitally rape the plaintiff;

(c) Mr Shakespeare would then anally rape the plaintiff;

(d) Mr Shakespeare would insist that he and the plaintiff took walks around the property, which the plaintiff now realises was so that nobody could see what was happening;

(e) The first time Mr Shakespeare raped the plaintiff, he took the plaintiff down to the end of Campbell Park School.

Sexual abuse by Mr Holt against the plaintiff

64. On dates that he does not now recall, but while he resided at Campbell Park, the plaintiff was sexually abused by a male teacher named Mr Holt.

Particulars of abuse

(a) Mr Holt preyed upon young boys (including the plaintiff) and at every opportunity would isolate the plaintiff;

(b) On these occasions, Mr Holt would inappropriately touch the plaintiff and fondle the plaintiff's genital area;

(c) In addition to the abuse referred to in subparagraph (b) above, Mr Holt would anally rape the plaintiff.

Sexual abuse by Miss Savage against the plaintiff

65. On a date that he does not now recall, the plaintiff was sexually abused by a female staff member at Campbell Park named Miss Savage.

Particulars of abuse

(a) On one occasion, on a date that the plaintiff does not now recall, he was taken by Miss Savage into Miss Savage's bedroom;

(b) Miss Savage told the plaintiff to take off his trousers and then performed oral sex on the plaintiff;

(c)   In addition to the abuse referred to in subparagraph (b) above, Miss Savage then engaged in sexual intercourse with the plaintiff.

Sexual abuse by Mrs Campbell against the plaintiff

66.   On a date that he does not now recall, but after 1975, while he resided at Campbell Park, the plaintiff was sexually abused by a female staff member named Mrs Campbell, who was an older woman.

Particulars of abuse

(a)   On one occasion, Mrs Campbell approached the plaintiff and fondled his genitals and commented about the size of his penis.

Sexual abuse by Mrs Johnson against the plaintiff

67.   On dates that he does not now recall, but while he resided at Campbell Park, the plaintiff was sexually propositioned by a female teacher named Mrs Johnson.

Particulars of abuse

(a)   On regular occasions, on dates the plaintiff does not now recall, he was approached by Mrs Johnson, who asked the plaintiff if the plaintiff wanted to have sexual intercourse with her;

(b)   On a number of occasions, the plaintiff was taken by Mrs Johnson to her house in the village, and made to have sexual intercourse with her.

Sexual abuse by Mr Johnson against the plaintiff

68.   On dates that he does not now recall, but while he resided at Campbell Park, the plaintiff was sexually abused by Mrs Johnson's husband, Mr Johnson, who was regularly at Campbell Park, although the plaintiff does not know if he was a staff member.

Particulars of abuse

(a) On several occasions, commencing at about 12 November 1974, after he had been in Dunedin Hospital for an operation on his nose, Mr Johnson returned the plaintiff to Campbell Park by car;

(b) On the way to Campbell Park, Mr Johnson took the plaintiff to a shed on the school property and anally raped the plaintiff;

(c) Mr Johnson would also come into the dormitory at night and anally rape the plaintiff;

(d) In addition, Mr Johnson would enter the dormitory during the day if the plaintiff was sick in bed and anally rape the plaintiff;

(e) Mr Johnson was physically violent and very cruel to the plaintiff during the periods when he sexually abused the plaintiff, in that he would physically shove the plaintiff to the ground before raping him.

Sexual abuse by Mr Willis against the plaintiff

69. On dates that he does not now recall, the plaintiff was sexually abused by the Principal of Campbell Park School, Mr Willis.

Particulars of abuse

(a) About once a week, Mr Willis would take the plaintiff to his own office, ostensibly for discussions about the plaintiff's progression of his education;

(b) During these visits, Mr Willis would make the plaintiff pull down his trousers and perform sexual acts on him;

(c) Mr Willis would play with the plaintiff's penis and make the plaintiff lean over his desk;

(d) Mr Willis would then anally rape the plaintiff.

Particulars of abuse

(a) Mr O'Connor would perform oral sex on the plaintiff, and make the plaintiff perform oral sex on him;

(b) In addition, Mr O'Connor would take the plaintiff to his motor home, force the plaintiff on to the bed and anally rape the plaintiff;

(c) Mr O'Connor (and the other male staff members identified by the plaintiff as sexual abusers) would also sexually abuse the plaintiff, in the manner referred to in (a) and (b) above, in the graveyard.

Sexual abuse by Mr Medcalf against the plaintiff

73. On dates that he does not now recall, but while he resided at Campbell Park, the plaintiff was sexually abused by a male housemaster named Mr Medcalf.

Particulars of abuse

(a) Mr Medcalf sexually abused the plaintiff on a number of occasions, at his home or at the gym or the dorm;

(b) The sexual abuse consisted of kissing and anal rape.

Sexual abuse by Mrs Joan Gibbons against the plaintiff

74. On dates that he does not now recall, but while he resided at Campbell Park, the plaintiff was sexually abused by a female staff member named Mrs Joan Gibbons.

Particulars of abuse

(a) Mrs Joan Gibbons "liked" young boys, including the plaintiff and would force him to have sex with her.

Sexual abuse by Mr Malees against the plaintiff

75. On dates that he does not now recall, but while he resided at Campbell Park's Disney House, the plaintiff was sexually abused by

an overweight male staff member whose name the plaintiff believes was Mr Matees.

Particulars of abuse

(a)   Mr Matees would approach the plaintiff and start to fondle the plaintiff on his genital area;

(b)   On some occasions, on dates the plaintiff does not now recall, Mr Matees would take the plaintiff into the TV room and remove the plaintiff's pyjama trousers;

(c)   Mr Matees would then perform oral sex on the plaintiff;

(d)   On other occasions, the sexual assaults as described in subparagraphs (b) and (c) above would take place in the outside toilets.

Sexual abuse by Mr Parsons against the plaintiff

76.   On dates that he does not now recall, but while he resided at Campbell Park, the plaintiff was sexually abused by a housemaster named Mr Parsons.

Particulars of abuse

(a)   Mr Parsons would take the plaintiff out into the bush on the pretext of teaching the plaintiff survival skills;

(b)   Mr Parsons would then force the plaintiff to perform oral sex on him and would perform oral sex on the plaintiff.

Campbell Park: physical assaults

77.   On dates that he does not now recall, but on regular occasions, the plaintiff was hosed down in the middle of winter as punishment by a staff member, Mr Bernie Welsh.

78.   The plaintiff was physically abused on a daily basis while he resided at Campbell Park. The most common form of physical abuse was the use of fists and hitting to the plaintiff's body. The perpetrators of the abuse were Mrs Johnson, Mr Bernie Welsh, Mrs Joan Gibbons, Mr Pat Welsh, Mr O'Connor, Mr Wiering and Mr Matees.

31

Campbell Park: assaults by other boys

79. Staff at Campbell Park permitted and/or failed to prevent, other residents from assaulting, or threatening assaults, against the plaintiff. The plaintiff was repeatedly beaten and physically assaulted by other boys, without intervention by staff members. Staff members, whose names the plaintiff cannot now remember, were present when the assaults referred to in the paragraphs below took place but omitted to take any action to prevent the assaults, or to adequately punish, or educate the offenders about the negative effects of violence. In addition, the plaintiff was not provided with any help to deal with the effects of the abuse.

80. On the date that he first arrived at Campbell Park, the plaintiff was subjected to an "initiation ceremony" by the other boys at Campbell Park. This consisted of the plaintiff being held down with a blanket over his body and anally raped.

81. The plaintiff was repeatedly anally raped by other boys at Campbell Park. A lot of the sexual abuse the plaintiff suffered from the other boys at Campbell Park took place in "the cave."

82. The older boys at Campbell Park also anally raped the plaintiff (and other boys) at the graveyard which was on a hill behind Campbell Park School.

83. The plaintiff was physically beaten and anally raped by older boys at the flying fox area at Campbell Park, because this was out of bounds and therefore away from staff members.

84. The plaintiff was anally raped by other boys in the swimming pool and changing rooms, which were also out of bounds for the boys when not in use.

85. Older boys also used to bully and anally rape the plaintiff (and other boys) in the gymnasium.

86. On dates that he does not now recall, but while he resided at Campbell Park, the plaintiff was sexually abused by an older boy at Taylor House named Jason Q. The abuse mainly took place in the plaintiff's room. Jason Q forced the plaintiff to perform oral sex on him and anally raped the plaintiff.

87. During the sexual assaults referred to in the paragraph above, Jason Q threatened the plaintiff with severe beatings if the plaintiff did not acquiesce to his demands. Jason Q would also make sexual advances to the plaintiff in the TV room.

Campbell Park: witnessing of assaults

88. The plaintiff witnessed other boys being bullied, physically assaulted, beaten, punched and kicked by other boys and/or staff members. Staff members, whose names the plaintiff cannot now recall, allowed these assaults to take place by physically assaulting boys themselves, omitting to take any action to prevent the assaults, or to adequately punish, or educate the offenders about the negative effects of violence and by omitting to take adequate action when boys reported incidents of physical assaults. In addition, no measures were put in place to protect the plaintiff and other boys who were the victims of physical assaults from their offenders. Staff members also failed to provide the plaintiff and other boys with any help to deal with the effects of the physical assaults.

89. On dates that he does not now recall, but on regular occasions while he resided at Campbell Park, the plaintiff witnessed another boy at Campbell Park named Barry Ryder being sexually abused by another boy named Stuart Ellwood in the garden area of the school.

90. On dates that he does not now recall, but on regular occasions while he resided at Campbell Park, the plaintiff witnessed Barry Ryder being sexually abused by staff and bigger boys at Campbell Park, whose names the plaintiff does not now recall. The abuse consisted of Barry Ryder being dragged down to the trees and then raped.

91. On dates that he does not now recall, but on regular occasions while he resided at Campbell Park, the plaintiff witnessed another boy at Campbell Park named Kevin Froggatt being severely hit by Mr O'Connor and other staff members.

92. On dates that he does not now recall, the plaintiff witnessed another boy named Richard Evans having his genitals fondled and being sexually abused by Jason Q.

93. On dates that he does not now recall, but on at least two occasions when the plaintiff (and other boys) was being sent by bus to Lyttleton, to catch the ferry, the older boys would abuse the

younger boys on the ferry. The abuse occurred in the evenings. After staff members had left the boys to their own devices, the older boys would anally rape the plaintiff.

Campbell Park: inadequate monitoring

94. Throughout 1978, the plaintiff's school reports recorded that the plaintiff was being bullied by other boys at Campbell Park.

95. On 9 October 1978, Mr Willis, the Principal of Campbell Park, commented on the fact that the plaintiff had been involved in sexual misconduct with an older boy who was known by staff to be a molester of little girls and boys.

96. Despite the fact that Social Welfare staff and/or agents were clearly aware of the treatment the plaintiff was receiving, the plaintiff remained at Campbell Park until 12 December 1978.

97. Staff at Campbell Park did not take any steps to enquire into the conduct, talk to the boys involved, or offer the plaintiff any form of counselling.

Campbell Park: traumatic incidents

98. On dates that he does not now recall, but on regular occasions, the plaintiff was forced to carry bricks up and down the hill behind Taylor until the plaintiff was absolutely exhausted. The instigator of this was a staff member named Mr Wering.

Campbell Park: emotional abuse

99. The plaintiff was emotionally abused and verbally abused by staff members and other boys on a regular basis. The staff members allowed emotional and verbal abuse to occur by emotionally and verbally abusing boys themselves, and by omitting to take any action to prevent the abuse, or to adequately punish, or educate the offenders about the negative effects of emotional and verbal abuse.

100. On one occasion, on a date he does not now recall, a female staff member named Mrs Gibbons told the plaintiff that he was fat and withheld the plaintiff's pudding at dinner time.

108. On one occasion, on a date he does not now recall, but while he resided at Stanmore Road, the plaintiff was sexually abused by Mr Shakespeare, the staff member from Campbell Park referred to in paragraph 53 above. Mr Shakespeare had moved from Campbell Park to work at Stanmore Road while the plaintiff resided there.

109. The sexual assaults referred to in the paragraph above mainly consisted of oral sex.

Stanmore Road: assaults by other boys

110. Staff at Stanmore Road permitted and/or failed to prevent, other residents from assaulting, or threatening assaults, including sexual assaults, against the plaintiff. The plaintiff was repeatedly beaten and physically assaulted by other boys, without intervention by staff members. Staff members, whose names the plaintiff cannot now remember, were present when the assaults took place but omitted to take any action to prevent the assaults, or to adequately punish, or educate the offenders about the negative effects of violence. In addition, the plaintiff was not provided with any help to deal with the effects of the abuse.

111. On a date that he does not now specifically recall, but soon after he arrived at Stanmore Road, he suffered an "initiation" process at the Boys' Home.

Particulars of initiation process

(a) Other boys viciously beat the plaintiff;

(b) The plaintiff had a blanket thrown over his head and was then punched and kicked by boys who the plaintiff was unable to identify because of the blanket;

(c) Several boys then anally raped the plaintiff.

112. On dates that he does not now recall, but soon after he was transferred to Stanmore Road, the plaintiff was sexually abused by another boy at Stanmore Road named Steven Cross, who forced the plaintiff to perform oral sex on him.

113. On dates that he does not now recall, the plaintiff was anally raped by Steven Cross who also inappropriately fondled the plaintiff.

Campbell Park: witnessing of assaults

114. The plaintiff witnessed other boys being bullied, physically assaulted, beaten, punched and kicked by other boys and/or staff members. Staff members, whose names the plaintiff cannot now recall, allowed these assaults to take place by physically assaulting boys themselves, omitting to take any action to prevent the assaults, or to adequately punish, or educate the offenders about the negative effects of violence and by omitting to take adequate action when boys reported incidents of physical assaults. In addition, no measures were put in place to protect the plaintiff and other boys who were the victims of physical assaults from their offenders. Staff members also failed to provide the plaintiff and other boys with any help to deal with the effects of the physical assaults.

Stanmore Road: emotional abuse

115. The plaintiff was emotionally abused and verbally abused by staff members and other boys on a regular basis. The staff members allowed emotional and verbal abuse to occur by emotionally and verbally abusing boys themselves, and by omitting to take any action to prevent the abuse, or to adequately punish, or educate the offenders about the negative effects of emotional and verbal abuse.

Campbell Park, Stanmore Road: violent culture and "no narking"

116. The plaintiff was told by staff and boys that it was inappropriate to "nark", or in other words, there was a code of conduct that prevented a person from reporting abusive treatment by others and colleagues. The code of conduct was such that if the plaintiff did report abuse, he would suffer the consequences, namely the plaintiff would be severely beaten by other boys if he told. In any case, the plaintiff did not think that staff members would take any action to protect the plaintiff, as they had witnessed violence being perpetrated on the plaintiff without taking any action and they had also used violence themselves on the plaintiff.

117. The plaintiff was constantly exposed to violence at the Boys' Homes. The Director-General and his staff and/or agents, caused and/or allowed the plaintiff to be exposed to violence at the Boys' Homes by:

(a)   using and/or allowing the use of physical assaults;

(b)   omitting to take any action to prevent physical assaults, or to adequately punish offenders, or educate offenders about the negative effects of violence;

(c)   omitting to take action when boys reported incidents of physical assaults;

(d)   failing to provide adequate measures to protect boys from physical assaults or to separate the victims of physical assaults from their offenders; and

(e)   omitting to provide adequate help to victims of physical assaults.

Campbell Park, Stanmore Road: criminal culture and lack of schooling

118.   The plaintiff did not receive adequate education while at the Boys' Homes, but instead learned about criminal conduct and violence. The plaintiff was exposed to and learned about criminal conduct and activities, including how to steal, commit burglaries and break into houses, from other residents at the Boys' Homes on a daily basis, without intervention from staff members, whose names the plaintiff cannot now recall, who were often present when criminal conduct was discussed. The Director-General and his staff and/or agents allowed the plaintiff to be exposed to and learn criminal conduct and activities by:

(a)   omitting to take action to prevent the plaintiff and other boys from discussing criminal conduct and activities;

(b)   failing to provide education about the negative effects of crime, or to teach the plaintiff and other boys that criminal behavior was wrong; and

(d)   allowing the plaintiff to live with and mix with other young criminals.

Inappropriate monitoring of care and living arrangements

119.   The Director-General and/or his agents, were monitoring the progress and placement of the plaintiff while he was a minor.

Templeton Hospital: sexual abuse

127. On a date that he does not now specifically recall, but soon after his admission in December to Templeton Hospital, the plaintiff was sexually abused by two Pakeha male staff members in their 20s or 30s, whose names the plaintiff does not now remember, but who lived at the back of the kitchen at Templeton Hospital.

128. The sexual abuse referred to in paragraph 127 above consisted of inappropriate fondling, masturbation, oral sex and attempted anal rape.

Templeton Hospital: physical abuse

129. On a date that he does not now recall, but during his December admission to Templeton Hospital, the plaintiff believes he was physically abused, in the swimming pool, by staff members whose names the plaintiff does not now recall.

130. As a result of the incident referred to in paragraph 129 above, the plaintiff is deeply afraid of water, and even taking a shower causes the plaintiff to feel terrified. The plaintiff remembers that the staff members were Pakeha, both male and female and in their 20s or 30s.

Templeton Hospital: traumatic incidents

131. On dates that he does not now recall, but while he was a patient at Templeton Hospital, the plaintiff (and other patients at Templeton Hospital) was forced by the Head Matron at Templeton Hospital to eat dirt as punishment.

132. On dates that he does not now recall, but on regular occasions while he was a patient at Templeton Hospital, the plaintiff and other boys were forced by staff members, whose names the plaintiff cannot now recall, to hit each other while they were waiting for breakfast.

Templeton Hospital: failure to develop life skills

133. Because of the failure of the Board to provide the plaintiff with a functional, therapeutic environment while he was a psychiatric patient, the plaintiff did not develop the necessary personal skills

133. and resources to enable him to deal with the ordinary demands of
adult life in a reasonable manner.

Damage

134. As a result of the facts referred to in paragraphs 59 - 125 in relation
to abuse suffered while the plaintiff was in Social Welfare care; and
paragraphs 127 – 133 in relation to abuse suffered while the
plaintiff was a patient at Templeton Hospital, the plaintiff has
suffered damage and loss, which is ongoing.

Particulars

(a) The plaintiff finds it impossible to have a relationship with
anybody, because the plaintiff has a complete inability to
trust;

(b) The plaintiff finds it difficult to sleep and suffers from
nightmares about his experiences;

(c) The plaintiff suffers from depression;

(d) The plaintiff has anxiety attacks;

(e) The plaintiff finds it very difficult to revisit his experiences
and finds even the litigation process and just talking about
what happened, very stressful;

(f) The plaintiff has suffered from alcohol and drug addiction as
a coping mechanism;

(g) The plaintiff has attempted to commit suicide on several
occasions.

LETTERS FROM MEMBERS OF THE NEW ZEALAND GOVERNMENT TO GET HELP FOR THE ABUSE I SUFFERED HAS A CHILD HAS A STATE WARD A LOT OF THEM PASS THE BUCK ON TO OTHERS MEMBERS OF PARLIEMENT

Letter from the Office of Hon Christopher Finlayson

 Office of Hon Christopher Finlayson

Attorney-General
(includes responsibility for Serious Fraud Office)
Minister for Treaty of Waitangi Negotiations
Minister for Arts, Culture and Heritage

2 SEP 2009

Darryl W Smith
33 Kana St
MATAURA 9712

Dear Mr Smith

Thank you for your letter of 7 August 2009.

There are two things that the Government has done that may assist you.

First, the Ministry of Social Development has a Historic Claims Unit established which you can contact direct to raise your concerns. You can contact them at:

Historic Claims Unit
Ministry of Social Development
PO Box 1556
Wellington

This Unit investigates claims and can provide settlement of claims, including an apology and compensation, after investigation. The Unit can also help you to get other forms of assistance.

Also, the Government has set up a Listening and Assistance Service, which is a forum for people who allege abuse or neglect or who have any concerns about their time in State care before 1992 to speak in confidence to a panel, chaired by Judge Carolyn Henwood. The Service can offer assistance, but not an apology or compensation.

If you wish to contact the Service you can do so at:

Confidential Listening and Assistance Service
PO Box 5939
Wellington
Phone: 0800-356-567
Email: info@listening.govt.nz

Yours sincerely

Hon Christopher Finlayson
Attorney-General

Letter from the Office of the Prime Minister

 Office of the Prime Minister

30 August 2007

Darryl W Smith
33 Kana Street
Mataura
SOUTHLAND

Dear Darryl W Smith

I am writing on behalf of the Prime Minister, Helen Clark, to thank you for your letter of 24 August 2007.

As the matter you have raised falls within the portfolio of the Associate Minister for Social Development and Employment (CYFS), Helen Clark has asked me to forward your letter to her colleague for consideration.

Yours sincerely

Dinah Okeby
Private Secretary

Letter from the Office of Annette King

House Bag 18041
Wellington 6160
New Zealand

Reference: 8000502

26 August 2009

Mr D W Smith
33 Kana Street
Mataura
SOUTHLAND

Dear Darryl

Thank you for your letter of 12 August 2009 requesting a letter of support to Hon Chris Finlayson, Attorney General, for compensation and rehabilitation after the United Nations Committee Against Torture released its conclusions and recommendations.

I understand Hon David Parker, Labour's Shadow Attorney General, will be responding on behalf of the Labour Caucus.

Thank you for writing.

Yours sincerely

Hon Annette King
Deputy Leader of the Labour Party
MP for Rongotai including the Chatham Islands

Parliament Buildings: email A.King@parliament.govt.nz / phone: +64 (0)4 817 9103
Electorate Office: email kingrmaa@xtra.co.nz / phone: +64 (0)4 387 3587
Website www.labour.org.nz

Letter from the Office of Lianne Dalziel

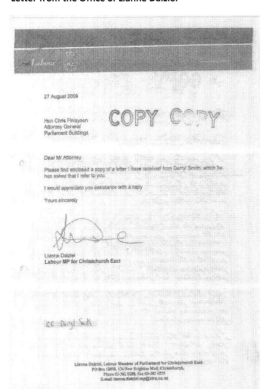

27 August 2009

Hon Chris Finlayson
Attorney General
Parliament Buildings

COPY COPY

Dear Mr Attorney

Please find enclosed a copy of a letter I have received from Darryl Smith, which he has asked that I refer to you.

I would appreciate you assistance with a reply.

Yours sincerely

Lianne Dalziel
Labour MP for Christchurch East

cc Darryl Smith

Lianne Dalziel, Labour Member of Parliament for Christchurch East
PO Box 13898, 156 New Brighton Mall, Christchurch,
Phone 03-382 0288, Fax 03-382 0255
E-mail lianne.dalziel.mp@xtra.co.nz

Letter from the office of Hon Ruth Dyson

Office of Hon Ruth Dyson
Minister of Labour
Minister for ACC
Minister for Senior Citizens
Minister for Disability Issues
Associate Minister for Social Development and Employment (Child, Youth & Family Services)
MP for Banks Peninsula

MIN/07/16#001

24 SEP 2007

Mr Darryl W Smith
33 Kana Street
Mataura
SOUTHLAND

Dear Mr Smith

Thank you for your letter that I received on 24 August 2007. The Prime Minister, Rt Hon Helen Clark, has also forwarded to me your letter that she received on 27 August 2007, asking that I reply on her behalf.

I understand from the Ministry of Social Development that you have been in contact with Garth Young, the National Manager Historic Claims, over the same issues as you discuss with me. I gather that you and Mr Young have talked about the potential mutual benefits of meeting to further discuss your complaints. I would certainly endorse that as being a very helpful starting point.

You suggest that I might meet with you and help you to get compensation and an apology. While it is not appropriate for me as Minister to intervene on your behalf, I have set clear expectations of the Ministry that every claim and historic complaint will be dealt with fairly.

As I am sure Mr Young has discussed with you, the Ministry tries to work directly with people who say they were subject to abuse or neglect in the past to resolve their claims fairly. This usually happens by the Ministry talking to the person about what they believe happened to them, and what they are seeking. Where they want compensation, the claim is investigated. Where the Ministry or its predecessors have got it wrong, it apologises and offers compensation based on what the Courts would award.

The Ministry may also offer other help to the person and their family. I know that, regardless of any discussion of your claim, they would as a priority look to help you and your family with your current situation.

Letter from the Office of The Prime Minister

 Office of the Prime Minister

8 January 2003

Darryl Smith
Private Bag 4726
Templeton
CHRISTCHURCH

Dear Darryl Smith

I am writing on behalf of the Prime Minister, to acknowledge your letter dated 30 December 2002.

Your letter has been placed before Helen Clark for her information.

Thank you for writing.

Yours sincerely

Dinah Okeby
Private Secretary

Letter from the Office of Hon Ruth Dyson

Office of Hon Ruth Dyson
Minister of Labour
Minister for ACC
Minister for Senior Citizens
Minister for Disability Issues
Associate Minister for Social Development and Employment (Child, Youth & Family Services)
MP for Banks Peninsula

15 February 2007   Reference: 02211

Darryl W Smith
Founder President & Victim
The National Centre for Missing &
Abused Children
PO Box 16849
Hornby 8004
CHRISTCHURCH

Dear Mr Smith

Thank you for your letter received on 15 February 2007 to Hon Ruth Dyson about
compensation.

Hon Ruth Dyson, Associate Minister for Social Development and Employment (Child,
Youth and Family) has asked for information from Child, Youth and Family and she will
respond to you once this has been received.

Yours sincerely

Lynda Little
Private Secretary (Child, Youth and Family)
Office of Hon Ruth Dyson

Letter from the Office of Hon Jim Anderton MP

Office of Hon Jim Anderton

Minister for Economic Development, Minister for Industry and Regional Development
Associate Minister of Health, Minister responsible for Public Trust

2 0 JAN 2003

Darryl Smith
Private Bag 4726
Templeton
Christchurch

Dear Darryl Smith

I am writing to acknowledge your two letters of 28 and 30 December concerning sexual abuse when you were a child.

I have the greatest personal sympathy for you, and can understand the anguish that a trauma such as this can cause to a child and throughout later life. However, as a Minister there are no practical steps I can take to obtain either an apology for you from the Ministry of Health or monetary compensation. These are things that lie outside my statutory powers.

I note however that you are intending to approach the Police and to ask them to look into the events in question. I think that this would be a worthwhile step; at least you would have the satisfaction of knowing that at the very least your concerns had been investigated, and there is always the possibility that a prosecution might follow. Should you decide to take that approach it would also be advisable, in my estimation, for you to take some independent legal advice.

I am sorry that I can't do anything more concrete to assist.

With best wishes
Yours sincerely

Jim Anderton
M P for Wigram and Leader of the Progressive Party

Parliament Buildings, Wellington, New Zealand. Telephone: (04) 471 9031. Facsimile: (04) 495 8441
Email: Jim.Anderton@parliament.govt.nz

Letter from the Office of Hon Dr Muriel Newman MP ACT New Zealand Whip

DR MURIEL NEWMAN MP
WELFARE, POLICE & ASSOC HEALTH SPOKESMAN
ACT NEW ZEALAND

21 February 2003

Darryl W Smith
Private Bag 4726
Templeton
Christchurch

Dear Darryl

Thank you for your letter of 3 February regarding your wish for an official apology and compensation.

It would be helpful for you to write me another letter providing me with details regarding the alleged incidents, and your sentence, by way of background information so that we can progress your request with all of the relevant details. If you give me permission I will forward the letter to the Minister.

I look forward to hearing from you soon.

Kindest regards

Dr Muriel Newman MP
ACT New Zealand Whip

Dr Muriel Newman MP, ACT New Zealand
Parliament Buildings WELLINGTON
Telephone: 04 4704653   Fax: 04 473 3720
Email: nzk.hall@parliament.govt.nz

Letter from the Office of Craig McNair

17 February 2003

Daryl W Smith
Private Bag 4726
Templeton
CHRISTCHURCH

Dear Daryl

Thankyou for your letter February 3, 2003.

I regret any feeling of wrong doing received by yourself over the period you stated.
The Minister in charge of Social Services is the Hon Steve Maharey.

This is the department that should address the problems you have raised.

Regards

Craig McNair MP
New Zealand First

CRAIG McNAIR MP
NEW ZEALAND FIRST
Parliament Buildings, Wellington
Telephone (04) 470-6574 Facsimile (04)
Email craig.mcnair@parliament.govt.nz

Letter from the Office of Hon Steve Mahaney

 Office of Hon Steve Maharey, M.P. for Palmerston North
Minister of Social Services and Employment
Minister of Broadcasting
Associate Minister of Education (Tertiary Education)
Minister responsible for Tertiary Education Commission

10 March 2003

Darryl Smith
Christchurch Prison
Private Bag 4726
Templeton
Christchurch

Dear Darryl Smith

On behalf of Hon Steve Maharey, Minister of Social Services and Employment, thank you for your letter of 3 February 2003 regarding compensation for allegations of abuse.

The matter you have raised falls within the portfolio responsibilities of the Associate Minister of Social Services and Employment. I have therefore referred your letter to Hon Ruth Dyson for her consideration.

Yours sincerely

Cherie Engelbrecht
Private Secretary (Child, Youth and Family)

Letter from the Office of Hon Georgia Beyer

NEW ZEALAND
Labour

11 March 2003

Darryl Smith
Private Bag 4726
Templeton
CHRISTCHURCH

Dear Darryl

On behalf of Georgina Beyer, MP for Wairarapa, I would like to thank you for your letter requesting compensation for past sufferings and apologise for the delay in responding.

Unfortunately, as Georgina's resources are limited, she only able to act on behalf of her own Wairarapa constituents, therefore she suggests that you contact your own MP.

The issues you have raised are very sensitive and Georgina feels they would be better dealt with by someone closer to you.

Yours sincerely

Jo Scddon
Electorate Agent to
GEORGINA BEYER MP

Georgina Beyer, Member of Parliament for Wairarapa
PO Box 913, Masterton. Phone 06-378 8736 Fax 06-378 1556
E-Mail gbeyer@wise.net.nz
PO Box 88, Dannevirke. Phone 06-374 7574 Fax 06-374 5708
Email g.beyer@xtra.co.nz

Parliament Buildings
Wellington, New Zealand
Phone +64 4 470 6632
Fax +64 4 472 6290
www. labour.org.nz

Letter from the office of Hon Trevor Malland

Hon Trevor Mallard
Minister of Education
Minister of State Services
Minister for Sport, Fitness and Leisure
Minister responsible for the Education Review Office
Associate Minister of Finance

14 February 2003

Darryl Smith
Private Bag 4726
Templeton
CHRISTCHURCH

Dear Darryl Smith

Thank you for your letter of 24 December 2002 concerning your claims against the Ministry of Education relating to your time at the former Campbell Park Boys School. I note that you also wrote to the Prime Minister, who has forwarded your letter to me.

I am advised by the Ministry of Education that you have also corresponded with them about the issues you raised with me and with the Prime Minister. The Ministry is currently preparing a response to your latest letter and you can expect a reply from them soon.

You have raised serious and complex legal and factual issues, and it will take some time to deal with them in an appropriate way. You have already been advised to seek the assistance of a lawyer to proceed with your claims and I reiterate this advice. If you wish to provide further information or communicate again on these matters I suggest that you or your lawyer write directly to the Ministry contact person who is Jan Breakwell, Manager Legal Services, Ministry of Education, P O Box 1666, Wellington.

Yours sincerely

Trevor Mallard
MINISTER OF EDUCATION

Letter from the Office of Lianne Dalziel

Hon Lianne Dalziel
Minister of Commerce
Minister of Immigration
Minister for Senior Citizens
Minister Responsible for the Law Commission
Associate Minister of Justice
Associate Minister of Education
Member of Parliament for Christchurch East

2 0 JAN 2003

Daryl Smith
Private Bag 4762
Templeton
CHRISTCHURCH

Dear Daryl Smith

On behalf of Hon Lianne Dalziel Associate Minister of Education I acknowledge your letter of 7 January 2003 concerning child abuse in the 1970s.

Your letter has been referred to Hon Ruth Dyson, Minister for Disability Issues, for her consideration and response.

Yours sincerely

Christine Druce
Private Secretary

Parliament Buildings, Wellington, New Zealand.
Email: www.labour.org.nz

Telephone: (04) 470 6562
Facsimile: (04) 495 8463

Letter from the Office of Hon Peter Dunn

United
Future
New Zealand

29 January 2003

Mr Darryl Smith
Private Bag 4726
Templeton
CHRISTCHURCH

Dear Mr Smith

Thank you for your correspondence received 13 January 2003.

In your letter you noted that you are currently seeking legal advice and have
yet to file a complaint with the Police. As this matter has yet to progress into
a formal complaint, it is not appropriate for me to take action by providing
you with support. This matter first needs to be thoroughly investigated and
a decision reached before an apology or compensation agreement can be
made.

I suggest that you continue to corroborate your information with the other
ex-pupils involved and seek appropriate advice to support your case being
investigated.

I wish you the best of luck with your case.

Yours sincerely

Hon Peter Dunne
**MP for Oharia-Belmont
Leader, United Future**

Focusing on Families
United Future New Zealand
Parliament Buildings, Wellington
Ph: (04) 471 9410 Fax: (04) 499 7266
Email: united.nz@parliament.govt.nz

NZ

Letter from the office of Hon Pete Hodgson

Office of Hon Pete Hodgson
MP for Dunedin North

Minister of Energy
Minister of Fisheries
Minister of Research, Science and Technology
Minister for Crown Research Institutes

Associate Minister for Industry
and Regional Development
Associate Minister of Foreign Affairs and Trade
Convenor, Ministerial Group on Climate Change

21 January 2003

Darryl Smith
Private Bag 4726
Templeton
CHRISTCHURCH

Dear Darryl Smith

Thank you for your letter of 4 January regarding Ministerial support in your quest for reparations from a series of government ministries.

While I have passed your letter on to the Minister, your correspondence is best addressed to the relevant Ministers responsible for these three ministries, namely Hon Steve Maharey, Hon Trevor Mallard and Hon Annette King, or your local MP.

Yours sincerely

Amelia Carter
Private Secretary to
Hon Pete Hodgson
MP for Dunedin North

Letter from the office of Hon Dr Michael Cullen

Office of Hon Dr Michael Cullen
Deputy Prime Minister
Minister of Finance
Minister of Revenue
Leader of the House of Representatives

11 February, 2003

Darryl W Smith
Private Bag 4726
Templeton
CHRISTCHURCH

Dear Darryl

On behalf of the Hon Dr Michael Cullen, Minister of Finance, thank you for your letter of 3 February 2003.

Your letter has been passed on to Dr Cullen for his information. However, as the issues you have raised, fall within the portfolio responsibilities of Hon Steve Maharey, I have referred a copy of your letter to him for his consideration.

Thank you for writing.

Yours sincerely

Katy Greco
Private Secretary

Letter from the office of Hon George Hawkins

 Office of Hon George Hawkins
Minister of Police
Minister of Internal Affairs
Minister of Civil Defence
Minister of Veterans' Affairs

7 February 2003

Darryl W Smith
Private Bag 4726
Fendalton
CHRISTCHURCH

Dear Mr Smith

On behalf of the Minister of Police, Hon George Hawkins, thank you for your
letter of 3 February 2003 concerning allegations of child abuse.

Your letter relates to matters which are the responsibility of the Commissioner
of Police. I have therefore referred your letter to his office for consideration.

Yours sincerely

Gerry Cunneen
Adviser (Police)

Letter from the office of Ruth Dyson and signed by the MP

 Office of Hon Ruth Dyson
Minister for ACC
Minister for Senior Citizens
Minister of Women's Affairs
Minister for Disability Issues
Associate Minister of Health
Associate Minister for Social Development and Employment (Child, Youth & Family Services)
MP for Banks Peninsula

24 MAR 2004

Mr Darryl Smith
Private Bag 3000
WANGANUI

Dear Mr Smith

Thank you for your letter of the 3 March 2004 and your comments and concern about children who have been in the state's care.

I am interested in any complaints you may have about children who may have been physically, emotionally or sexually abused while they were in care. Any such complaints should be followed up.

As a first step you should write to Zoe Griffiths, who is the Chief Legal Officer for Child, Youth and Family. Her address is Department of Child, Youth and Family Services, PO Box 2620, Wellington. She will be able to give you advice about how to file a statement of claim with the department and the information that needs to be included for the complaint to be investigated.

Thank you again for writing to me.

Yours Sincerely

Hon Ruth Dyson
Associate Minister for Social Development and Employment (Child, Youth and Family)

Letter from Hon Ruth Dyson

Office of Hon Ruth Dyson
Minister for ACC
Minister for Senior Citizens
Minister of Women's Affairs
Minister for Disability Issues
Associate Minister of Health
Associate Minister for Social Development and Employment (Child, Youth & Family Services)
MP for Banks Peninsula

Darryl Smith
Private Bag 3000
WANGANUI

8 March 2004   Our Ref: 00536

Dear Darryl Smith

Hon Ruth Dyson, Associate Minister for Social Development and Employment with responsibility for Child Youth and Family Services, has asked me to thank you for your letter dated 24 February 2004, regarding compensation.

Hon Ruth Dyson will give you feedback on this matter when it has been discussed with the Ministry.

Yours sincerely

Trish Dunlop
Ministerial Secretary/Assistant

Letter from Emma Campbell from the office of National MP Sarah Dowie

28th January 2015

D Smith
481A Yarrow Street
Glengarry
Invercargill 9810

Dear Darryl,

Thank you for coming to our office and advising us of the important issues you wish to highlight to the New Zealand Government and public.

I'm afraid it is not possible for you to speak directly to Parliament. However, you can write a letter to your Member of Parliament, Sarah Dowie formalising your concerns and wishes which can then be directed to the relevant Minister through this office.

We look forward to your correspondence.

Kind Regards,

Emma Campbell
Senior MP Support
Office of Sarah Dowie, Member of Parliament for Invercargill

Office of Sarah Dowie, Member of Parliament for Invercargill
Rothbury House, Level One, 36 Kelvin Street, PO Box 249, Invercargill
p 03 218 6813 | e Sarah.DowieMP@parliament.govt.nz

Letter from Tim Barnett office

MEMBER OF PARLIAMENT

Our Reference: LL3867C

11 March, 2004

Daryl W Smith
Paparua Prison
Private Bag 4726
Templeton

Dear Daryl,

CYFS Issues

Further to your request for information, we have now received a reply from the Associate Minister for Social Development and Employment, the Hon. Ruth Dyson. We apologise for the delay but there had a been a reshuffle of portfolio's for Minister,'s and it appears our original letter to Hon. Steve Maharey was mislaid.

However, I now enclose a copy of the reply from the new Minister and this will enable you to take the appropriate action that you think is suitable for your circumstances.

Once again, we apologise for the delay.

Yours sincerely,

Lynne Latham
Electorate Office Caseworker

Electorate Office **Parliament Buildings**

Please quote the reference number at the top of the page when responding to this correspondence.
Thank you.

CHRISTCHURCH CENTRAL   Labour

Letter from ACT Party with list of MPs to write too

January 9, 2003

Darryl W. Smith
Private Bag 4726
Templeton
Christchurch

ACT NEW ZEALAND
Promoting freedom, choice
and responsibility
www.act.org.nz

Level 1, Block B
Westfield New Zealand Building
Nutfield Street
P O Box 99851
Newmarket
Auckland

Phone: (09) 3230470
Fax: (09) 3230472
E-mail: info@voteact.org.nz

Dear Darryl

ACT currently has nine MP's in Parliament. They are as follows:

- Richard Prebble CBE (Leader)
- Ken Shirley (Deputy Leader)
- Rodney Hide
- Dr. Muriel Newman
- Stephen Franks
- Donna Awatere Huata
- Gerry Eckhoff
- Deborah Coddington
- Heather Roy

If you have any further queries regarding the party don't hesitate to contact me.

Kind regards

Andrea Kennedy
Electorate Agent
ACT New Zealand

Letter from John Hayes National MP

JOHN HAYES
Member of Parliament for Wairarapa

2 September 2009

Darryl W Smith
33 Kana Street
Mataura
Southland

Dear Mr Smith

Thank you for your letter of 21 August 2009. I appreciate your views and correspondence.

While it would be inappropriate for me to look into the concerns you raised, I have taken the liberty of forwarding your letter to Hon Bill English. As your local MP, I am confident that Hon Bill English will endeavour to respond to your correspondence.

I wish you all the best and thank you again for your correspondence.

Yours sincerely

John Hayes
MP for Wairarapa

Parliament Buildings   direct dial: +64 4 471 9926
Wellington   facsimile: +64 4 817 6596
New Zealand   email: john.hayes@parliament.govt.nz

National

62 Queen Street   direct dial: +64 6 370 1213
PO Box 964   facsimile: +64 6 370 1214
Masterton   cell free: 0800 3 (SAYES)
                   email: johnhayes.mp@pbs.co.nz

Letter from Jo Foodhew National MP

Jo Goodhew
Member of Parliament for Rangitata

Darryl W. Smith
33 Kana Street
Mataura
Southland

27 August 2009

Dear Mr Smith,

Thank you very much for your letter dated 21 August 2009 regarding adequate compensation and rehabilitation that has been recommended by the United Nations Committee against Torture.

I have received advice from Hon. Chris Finlayson's office that he is working through the issues that you raised in your letter and that he will deal directly with you regarding these issues.

I want to wish you all the best with your questions and I hope you get the outcome you desire.

Yours sincerely

Jo Goodhew
MP for Rangitata

National

Parliament Buildings, Wellington 6160, New Zealand tel 04 817 8879 fax 04-839 0447 email jo.goodhew@national.org.nz

Letter from Amy Adams MP for Selwyn

Amy Adams
Member of Parliament for Selwyn

18 August 2009

Mr Darryl W Smith
33 Kana Street
Mataura
SOUTHLAND 9712

Dear Mr Smith,

Thank you for your letter of 10 August 2009.

I notice in your letter you advise you are also writing to other Members of Parliament, including your local MP, Hon Bill English, which I am pleased to hear as he is the most appropriate person to help with your complaint.

I appreciate you taking the time to write.

Yours sincerely

Amy Adams
MP for Selwyn

Parliament Buildings   tel +64 4 817 8201   620 Main South Road   ph +64 3 344 0418
Wellington 6160   fax +64 4 473 0488   Templeton   fax +64 3 344 0430
                          email amy.adams@parliament.govt.nz   Christchurch 8042   email addsqwill@parliament.govt.nz

National
www.national.org.nz

Letter from the office of Hon Patsy Wong

Office of Hon Pansy Wong

MP for Botany
Minister for Ethnic Affairs
Minister of Women's Affairs
Associate Minister for ACC

Associate Minister for Disability Issues
Associate Minister of Energy and Resources

1 6 DEC 2009

MIN 09/1908

Mr Darryl W Smith
33 Kana Street
MATAURA 9712

Dear Mr Smith

Thank you for your email to Hon Simon Power of 8 October 2009 in which you discussed your Work and Income Invalids benefit and ACC Independence allowance. I am responding to you as Associate Minister for ACC.

I have asked ACC for information on the matters you raise.

In February 2008, ACC assessed you for an Independence allowance and your Whole Person Impairment rating was found to be 35%. Because you had lodged your claim in November 1988, ACC backdated your independence allowance to that date. However, ACC has not paid you this entitlement for the time you were imprisoned from 10 December 2002 to 16 June 2003. This is in accordance with ACC's governing legislation which specifies that people cannot receive financial entitlements for time served in prison. You are currently receiving $481.13 every three months.

If you believe your impairment rating has changed since 2008, you can request a further assessment.

ACC has been in contact with Work and Income in regards to your invalids benefit. ACC was advised that you can contact Work and Income directly on 0800 999 009 to discuss possible options for further assistance.

Thank you again for writing. I hope my response clarifies this matter for you.

Yours sincerely

Hon Pansy Wong
Associate Minister for ACC

Private Bag 18041, Parliament Buildings, Wellington 6160, New Zealand. Telephone 64 4 817 6817 Facsimile 64 4 817 6517

Letter from Gerry Brownlee MP

GERRY BROWNLEE MP, Ilam

17 February 2003

Mr D W Smith
Private Bag 4726
Templeton
CHRISTCHURCH

Dear Mr Smith

Thank you for your letter received on 5 February 2003. Your letter alleges abuse from various government institutions.

The appropriate cause of action is the Police, with a view to laying charges against the abusers.

I wish you all the best.

Yours sincerely

pp

Gerry Brownlee
MP for Ilam

Letter from the Office of the Opposition

OFFICE OF THE LEADER OF THE OPPOSITION
House of Representatives

4 September 2007

Mr Darryl South
33 Kana Street
MATAURA 9712

Dear Mr Smith

On behalf of John Key, Leader of the Opposition, I acknowledge your letter received on 27 August regarding the abuse of former wards of the state.

Your points are noted. A copy of your letter has been forwarded on for the information of National's Welfare spokeswoman, Judith Collins.

Thank you for writing on this matter.

Yours sincerely

Sonia Beal
Correspondence Assistant

cc: Judith Collins

Parliament Buildings
Wellington
New Zealand

National

telephone +64 4 401 8839
facsimile +64 4 473 3976
website www.national.org.nz

LETTER FROM RT HON WINSTON PETERS

31 January 2003

Darryl W Smith
Private Bag 4726
Templeton
CHRISTCHURCH

Dear Mr Smith

Thank you for your letter of 28 December 2002 in which you seek assistance to obtain an apology and compensation.

Your intentions to lodge a complaint with the New Zealand Police is the correct course of action, and dependent upon their findings, it would then be appropriate to consider an apology or compensation.

I wish you well in your endeavours.

Yours sincerely

Rt Hon Winston Peters
MP for Tauranga
Leader New Zealand First

THE RT HON WINSTON PETERS MP
NEW ZEALAND FIRST LEADER
Parliament Buildings, Wellington
Telephone: (04) 471-9480 Facsimile: (04) 471-2042
Email: winston.peters@parliament.govt.nz

Letter from Russel Fairbrother MP for Napier

Parliament House
WELLINGTON 1.

NZ

Telephone (04) 471 9999

12 September 2003

Mr D W Smith
Private Bag 4726
Templeton
Christchurch

Dear Mr Smith

Thank you for your letter of 3 February regarding the abuse you suffered as a child while under state care.

I have forwarded your letter to Tim Barnett, Member of Parliament for Christchurch Central and your local Labour MP. His contact phone number is (03) 377 – 8840.

Yours sincerely

Russell Fairbrother
MP for Napier

Letter from Graham Capill Party Letter of Christan Heritage Party

12 February 2003

Mr Darryl Smith
Private Bag 4726
Templeton
CHRISTCHURCH

Dear Mr Smith

I was sorry to read about the abuse you suffered as a child. Some of what is now coming to light is appalling and inexcusable. It is even worse when a member of the church perpetrated the abuse.

As the CHP is not in parliament and does not have any MPs at the moment, we are not able to ask questions or put pressure on the government directly. I would suggest that the Ministerial portfolios you name would need more detail as to the nature of their involvement before they will accept responsibility for any breach of care. Why not write directly to them, outlining why you feel they failed you.

Sorry we cannot help you more. I can only point you to Jesus Christ, who although He was greatly wronged, died for our sins and forgave those who wronged Him. He knows your hurt and is able to heal the worst torment of the soul.

Yours sincerely

Graham Capill
PARTY LEADER

CHRISTIAN HERITAGE
PO Box 8088, Riccarton, Christchurch 8030
Ph. 03-384 2246 Fax 03-382 0456 Email info@chp.org.nz
VoNZ • Christian Coalition • Christian Democrats

Letter from Prime Minister Rt Hon John Key office on child abuse I suffered in state care

Office of the Prime Minister

Prime Minister
Minister of Tourism

Ministerial Services

Minister in Charge of the
NZ Security Intelligence Service
Minister Responsible for the GCSB

19 August 2009

Mr Darryl W Smith
33 Kana Street
Mataura
SOUTHLAND 9712

Dear Mr Smith

On behalf of the Prime Minister, Hon John Key, thank you for your letter dated
7 August 2009 concerning victims of child abuse.

As the issue you have raised falls within the portfolio responsibility of the
Minister for Social Development and Employment, Hon Paula Bennett, your
letter has been forwarded to that Minister's office for consideration.

Thank you for writing.

Yours sincerely

Briane Smith
Private Secretary

Private Bag 18041, Parliament Buildings, Wellington 6160 , New Zealand. Telephone 64 4 817 6800

Letter from Hon Peter Dunn United Future

UnitedFuture

18 August 2009

Mr Daryl Smith
33 Kana Street
Mataura 9712

Dear Mr Smith

Thank you for your letter of 10 August 2009 requesting that I approach the
Attorney-General on your behalf seeking an apology and compensation for
the sexual and physical abuse you suffered when in the care of the
Department of Social Welfare.

I will approach the Attorney-General accordingly and will let you know his
response in due course.

Yours sincerely

Hon Peter Dunne
MP for Ohariu
Leader of United Future

UnitedFuture New Zealand, Parliament Buildings, Wellington
Tel: +64 (04) 817 6827 Fax: +64 (04) 499 7266
www.unitedfuture.org.nz

Letter from Office of Hon Simon Power

Office of Hon Simon Power

MP for Rangitikei
Minister of Justice
Minister for State Owned Enterprises
Minister of Commerce

Minister Responsible for the Law Commission
Associate Minister of Finance
Deputy Leader of the House

14 September 2009

Mr Darryl W. Smith
33 Kana Street
Mataura
SOUTHLAND

Dear Mr Smith

The Hon Simon Power, Minister of Justice, has asked me to thank you for
your correspondence regarding recommendations of the United Nations
Committee Against Torture.

You will receive a reply as soon as possible.

Yours sincerely

Hannah McGregor
Justice Private Secretary
Office of the Minister of Justice
Hon Simon Power

Letter from the Office of Hon Murray McCully

Office of Hon Murray McCully
Minister of Foreign Affairs

3 September 2009

Darryl W. Smith
33 Kana Street
Mataura
Southland

Dear Darryl W. Smith

On behalf of Hon Murray McCully, Minister of Foreign Affairs, thank you for
your correspondence of 21 August.

The matter you have raised falls within the portfolio responsibilities of the
Minister of Justice. I have therefore referred your letter to Hon Simon Power
for his consideration.

Yours sincerely

Ashleigh Petley
Ministerial Secretary
Office of Hon Murray McCully

Letter from the office of Paula Bennett

Office of Hon Paula Bennett

MP for Waitakere
Minister for Social Development and Employment
Minister of Youth Affairs

1 September 2009

Darryl Smith
33 Kana Street
Mataura
SOUTHLAND

Dear Mr Smith

On behalf of the Minister for Social Development and Employment, Hon Paula Bennett, thank you for your letter of 21 August 2009 sent to the Minister and your letter of 7 August sent to the Prime Minister regarding your current claim for historical abuse while in State care.

Consideration is currently being given to the issues you have raised in your letter and you may expect a reply at the Minister's earliest convenience.

Yours sincerely

Jacinda Lean
Private Secretary – Child, Youth & Family
Office of Hon Paula Bennett
Minister for Social Development and Employment

Private Bag 18041, Parliament Buildings, Wellington 6160, New Zealand Telephone 64 4 817 6815 Facsimile 64 4 817 6515

Letter from the Office of Hon Tim Groser

Office of Hon Tim Groser

Minister of Trade
Minister of Conservation

Associate Minister of Foreign Affairs
Associate Minister for Climate Change Issues
(International Negotiations)

Ref: 09250

27 August 2009

Darryl W Smith
33 Kana Street
Mataura
SOUTHLAND

Dear Mr Smith

Thank you for your letter to Hon Tim Groser dated 21 August 2009, regarding a letter of support to Rt Hon Chris Finlayson.

Your letter has been passed on to the Minister for his information.

Yours sincerely

Fleur Thompson
Senior Private Secretary

Letter from the Office of Hon Nathan Guy

Office of Hon Nathan Guy

Minister of Internal Affairs
Associate Minister of Justice

Associate Minister of Transport
Minister Responsible for Archives New Zealand
Minister Responsible for the National Library

3 1 AUG 2009

Darryl Smith
33 Kana Street
Mataura
SOUTHLAND 9712

Dear Darryl

Hon Nathan Guy, Minister of Internal Affairs, has asked me to thank you for
your correspondence of 21 September 2009 about your request for a letter of
support to Hon Christopher Finlayson, Attorney-General.

The Minister is considering your letter, and you will receive a response shortly.

Yours sincerely

Andrew MacKenzie
Private Secretary

09/533

Letter from the Office of Paula Bennett

Office of Hon Paula Bennett
MP for Waitakere
Minister for Social Development and Employment
Minister of Youth Affairs

1 4 OCT 2009

Mr Darryl Smith
33 Kana Street
MATAURA

Dear Mr Smith

Thank you for your letters of 7 and 21 August 2009 to the Prime Minister, Hon John Key, and myself regarding the Government's response to people who have historic claims relating to their time in state care. The Prime Minister has asked that I reply to your letter to him, as the matters raised come within my responsibilities as Minister for Social Development and Employment.

I acknowledge your concerns about the current processes. The Attorney-General, Hon Chris Finlayson, recently announced that he is bringing forward a review of the way in which the Government is responding to these claims. This Government will seriously consider any recommendations that come out of the review.

In the meantime, I know that the Ministry of Social Development is committed to dealing with individual claims fairly. I understand the Ministry has previously invited you to meet with staff from the Care, Claims and Resolution team. That invitation remains open. 0508 326 459

Thank you for writing.

Yours sincerely

Hon Paula Bennett
Minister for Social Development and Employment

Private Bag 18041, Parliament Buildings, Wellington 6160, New Zealand. Telephone 64 4 817 6815 Facsimile 64 4 817 6513

Seeking support from The Governor General of New Zealand

GOVERNMENT HOUSE
New Zealand

7 February 2003

Mr Darryl W Smith
Private Bag 4726
Templeton
CHRISTCHURCH

Dear Mr W Smith

I am replying to your letter of 3 February to the Governor General concerning your wish to be compensated for being abused as a child. Dame Silvia is saddened to learn of the allegations you have made but is not in a position to assist you. I recommend you seek legal advice.

Yours sincerely

Hugo Judd
OFFICIAL SECRETARY

No justice for a life destroyed

By Chris Morris

1.   Wednesday, 19 July 2017

Victims of historic abuse in state care are fighting back, demanding justice - in cash and apologies - to help rebuild broken lives. But some are going further.In the second part of *ODT* Insight's special investigation, Chris Morris tells Darryl Smith's story.

MEDIA INFORMATION ON THE ABUSE AT CAMPBELL PARK SCHOOL

Darryl Smith says "blood money" is not enough to rebuild a life destroyed by sexual abuse in two countries.

The Dunedin man spent more than a decade in state care, in New Zealand and Australia, beginning as a 7-year-old boy in the early 1970s.

It was an experience that exposed him to sexual predators at one institution after another, including two run by the same Catholic order - the Brothers Hospitallers of St John of God.

And, despite receiving payouts and apologies on both sides of the Tasman, Mr Smith says it is not enough.

The 53-year-old wants justice in the form of a national inquiry and public apology from the New Zealand Government.

But he wants something more from the Church.

"I'm out to destroy them," Mr Smith told *ODT Insight*.

"They caused it all. It's their fault. If it wasn't for them in the first place, I wouldn't have gone down this road."

It is an anger that has been bubbling inside Mr Smith for more than 40 years, as childhood abuse led to adult criminal offending and, eventually, prison.

He still sleeps with the lights on, decades later, to keep the nightmares at bay. But, even today, an innocuous comment is enough to trigger a flashback.

MEDIA INFORMATION ON THE ABUSE AT CAMPBELL PARK SCHOOL

"Some of them them are quite horrific. Some days are better than others. Some days I can go with no nightmares at all.

"We [victims] are marked for the rest of our lives. To this day I still sit in the bath and I scrub myself raw, because of what happened."

- **Part 1: Delivered into the predators' hands**
- **Saint John of God response**
- **Roxburgh Health Camp**
- **Catholic Church**

It is a mark Mr Smith has carried since he was first targeted by an abusive brother from St John of God as a child in 1971.

He could not see it in the mirror, but it was clearly visible to the predators who preyed on the already vulnerable.

And every time he walked into a new state home, in Otago or elsewhere, the predators would turn their heads to look.

"I would put it like a pride of lions attacking young deer.

"Every time a little kid came in, you could see the lions and their faces starting to look with interest.

MEDIA INFORMATION ON THE ABUSE AT CAMPBELL PARK SCHOOL

"The first night there, you get blanketed, beaten up and raped by the older boys.

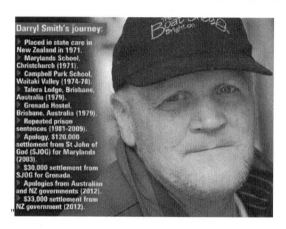

Darryl Smith's journey:
> Placed in state care in New Zealand in 1971.
> Marylands School, Christchurch (1971).
> Campbell Park School, Waitaki Valley (1974-78).
> Talera Lodge, Brisbane, Australia (1979).
> Grenada Hostel, Brisbane, Australia (1979).
> Repeated prison sentences (1981-2009).
> Apology, $120,000 settlement from St John of God (SJOG) for Marylands (2003).
> $30,000 settlement from SJOG for Grenada.
> Apologies from Australian and NZ governments (2012).
> $33,000 settlement from NZ government (2012).

Darryl Smith says "blood money" will never compensate for a childhood destroyed at Campbell Park School, in the Waitaki Valley, and other state care institutions. Photo: Gerard O'Brien

It was a childhood of torment that began as a 6-year-old with a mild intellectual disability, when he started running away from home.

Mr Smith put it down to a childhood "phase", but his parents were "struggling to cope".

MEDIA INFORMATION ON THE ABUSE AT CAMPBELL PARK SCHOOL

Eventually, when a Department of Education staff member suggested he go to Marylands School in Christchurch, they agreed.

The live-in facility catered for boys with intellectual and physical disabilities and behavioural problems, and his parents thought they were doing the right thing.

But their decision condemned him to life in what has become a notorious centre of historic sexual abuse, run by St John of God.

"I still remember playing on the floor with toys while my parents talked to this person from the department.

"I went in all right, but I came out completely different."

The school's problems hit the headlines decades later, when the first of 125 complaints alleging historic sexual abuse began to emerge.

The Catholic order eventually paid out $5.1 million to victims, and two of its brothers were convicted on historic sexual abuse charges after a police investigation.

MEDIA INFORMATION ON THE ABUSE AT CAMPBELL PARK SCHOOL

Darryl Smith as a boy at Campbell Park School. Photo: Supplied
One of them was Brother Rodger Moloney, who was jailed for his crimes in 2008.

Mr Smith said he was among Moloney's victims, but he was also targeted by other brothers and older boys at the school.

Mr Smith was moved from Marylands after nine months, first to Christchurch's Templeton Centre hospital and later to a series of State care institutions across New Zealand.

That eventually led to Campbell Park School, in the Waitaki Valley, beginning in 1974, where violence and sexual abuse by staff and older boys against younger boys was "rife", he said.

One of those to target Mr Smith was Peter Holdem, then one of the school's older boys but later, in 1986, to earn notoriety as the convicted killer of 6-year-old Louisa Damodran.

MEDIA INFORMATION ON THE ABUSE AT CAMPBELL PARK SCHOOL

"Everywhere I went, it was all the same stuff, just a different day. Everywhere I went in life I was getting hurt," Mr Smith said.

In 1979, aged 15, he joined his family in Australia, but was soon declared a state ward of Queensland.

He ended up in Talera Lodge, then run by the Queensland Baptists, where he was abused by a female staff member and raped by an older boy, he said.

Campbell Park School. Photo: supplied

A police investigation last year failed to identify the older boy and found the female staff member had died a decade earlier.

Later in 1979, Mr Smith was moved again, to Grenada Hostel in Brisbane, and found himself back in the care of St John of God.

More abuse followed, this time at the hands of Brother Bede Donnellan, he said.

"If I had known that ... I would never have gone there."

Donnellan - whose real name was John Donnellan - died in 1995, before facing justice, but the Church's Professional Standards Office in 2008 concluded "on the balance of probabilities" Donnellan had sexually assaulted Mr Smith.

But by then Mr Smith's childhood had led to a life of crime, and he was imprisoned repeatedly for theft and fraud offences between 1981 and 2009.

His experiences also drove a wedge between Mr Smith and his parents, who had refused to believe his claims of abuse as a child.

"When I told my parents 'this man touched me' ... I got a hiding."

Their estrangement continued until 2002, when his parents saw a television documentary detailing the abuses at Marylands.

Soon after, Mr Smith received a letter from his parents while in jail.

MEDIA INFORMATION ON THE ABUSE AT CAMPBELL PARK SCHOOL

"It said 'We finally believe you, Darryl'."

It was the start of a new life for Mr Smith, who vowed to stay out of prison and focus on seeking help and justice.

The following year, he received an apology and $120,000 in compensation from St John of God for his experiences at Marylands.

Six years later, after fighting St John of God over a second payout for his experiences in its care in Australia, the Catholic order relented and paid him a further $30,000.

In 2012, he also received apologies from the Australian and New Zealand Governments, and a $33,000 payment after speaking to New Zealand's Confidential Listening and Assistance Service.

He also participated in Australia's royal commission into child abuse, which offered "a wee bit of closure".

But that was still not enough for a childhood destroyed, Mr Smith said.

"It's destroyed me emotionally. It's given me a criminal record I didn't want. I've been robbed of everything."

As a result, Mr Smith remained a thorn in the church's side - emailing regularly and seeking additional settlements through an Australian lawyer, Peter Karp.

Mr Smith said payments to date were "blood money" and the sums involved "a total joke".

MEDIA INFORMATION ON THE ABUSE AT CAMPBELL PARK SCHOOL

A law change in Australia last year allowed abuse victims forced into unfair settlements to seek fresh payments, and Mr Smith planned to keep fighting.

He has also launched a series of petitions in New Zealand, including one calling on St John of God to pay for a lifetime of counselling and healthcare for all victims of Marylands.

He also wanted victims' criminal records wiped, and for the New Zealand Government to commit to a royal commission.

In the meantime, he has started a victim support group and is considering launching a political party to promote victims' rights.

But perhaps most audaciously, he is seeking fresh financial settlements for headline-grabbing amounts - including $5 million from SJOG and $1 billion from the Catholic Church itself - and has filed a complaint against SJOG with the International Criminal Court.

He has even written to the Vatican, asking to meet the Pope.

The only response to date has been from SJOG, which offered Mr Smith another 10 counselling sessions, free of charge.

The gesture, like anything SJOG could offer, was not enough for Mr Smith.

"To me, reimbursing me is giving me my life back, and they can't give me my life back, can they?"

Thankfully, Mr Smith has also found another outlet for his emotions - painting.

"Before I started art, I had like a black cloud around me. It's still there. I can get thunderstorms quite quickly ... but it's got blue sky there at the moment, just like outside."

chris.morris@odt.co.nz

MEDIA INFORMATION ON THE ABUSE AT CAMPBELL PARK SCHOOL

Unusual move to buy old school

By David Bruce

1.   Tuesday, 22 April 2014

Darryl Smith admits it is "very unusual" - a former old boy sexually abused while at Campbell Park Special School now leading a campaign to buy the Waitaki Valley property back into New Zealand ownership.

He has set up the Campbell Park Old Boys Committee, which would eventually become a trust, to raise up to $50 million to buy the 231ha estate from the Campbell Park Corporation, whose sole shareholder and director is American Charles Tomkins, now living in Australia.

A pupil from 1974 to 1978 at Campbell Park, a boarding school for children with behavioural or learning difficulties, he described it as "a very evil place". He was bullied and raped by other boys at the school.

"I have to admit it's very unusual for a child abused there to want to buy it," he told the *Otago Daily Times* yesterday. "But, I've been talking to people about it and they have said 'Why not'."

MEDIA INFORMATION ON THE ABUSE AT CAMPBELL PARK SCHOOL

Mr Smith tried contacting the owners of the property in an attempt to get information and discuss a possible sale, but had no response.

Mr Tomkin's son Nathan, who lives at and manages Campbell Park, did not return calls from the *Otago Daily Times* yesterday.

The property was on the market in 2008, when it had a capital rateable value of $3,3 million with the Waitaki District Council, through CBRE real estate agent Mike Beresford, but there was little interest.

Yesterday, Mr Beresford said Campbell Park was "not officially on the market", but inquiries could "reignite interest".

Mr Smith confirmed there had been no verbal offer from his committee in terms of the property.

The replacement value of Campbell Park had been estimated at $25 million, but up to $50 million could be needed to buy, improve and maintain it.

It would then be used as a residential refuge for adults with special needs, although some of the land and buildings, such as former staff homes, could be sold or leased.

Fundraising had just started, so when money was available it was planned to turn the committee into a charitable trust. Campbell Park was a boys' school from 1908 to 1988 when the Government sold it to Campbell Park Corporation.

Since then there had been a number of proposals for the property, including a school for American children.

It has a range of buildings, including a cave-house used by original owner William Dansey and the castle-like historic homestead later built by Robert Campbell.

MEDIA INFORMATION ON THE ABUSE AT CAMPBELL PARK SCHOOL

Surrounding the homestead is a 200-seat restaurant complex, a 225-seat theatre and accommodation for up to 300 people.

There are six classrooms, a library, arts and crafts rooms and technology centre, a well-equipped sports centre with a covered swimming pool, modern indoor gymnasium, tennis courts and sports fields, extensive equestrian facilities and a 1500m grass airstrip.

The second part comprises 32 homes in a village setting, including 10 three-bedroom villas, five 1940s hardwood three-bedroom homes, four Oamaru stone three-bedroom homes, 13 brick three and four-bedroom homes, as well as a 230sq m clubhouse. david.bruce@odt.co.nz

MEDIA INFORMATION ON THE ABUSE AT CAMPBELL PARK SCHOOL

Campbell Park ex pupils tell of abuse

19 Feb, 2004 1:34pm

A growing number of former Campbell Park School pupils are coming forward with stories of the abuse they suffered there. Wellington lawyer Sonja Cooper said she had already heard from 10 or 11 men who had attended the Otekaieke school. When the abuse allegations became public last month she had spoken to five ex-pupils. As media coverage of trouble at the institution continued, more contacted her. Ms Cooper said none of them had spoken to the others about what had happened at Campbell Park in the 1950s and 1960s, when it was a special school for boys considered "intellectually impaired" or who had caused difficulties at regular schools.

MEDIA INFORMATION ON THE ABUSE AT CAMPBELL PARK SCHOOL

"It's not like they all clubbed together. Their credibility is that they are coming from disparate parts of New Zealand." One of them lived in Australia. She said she was preparing their cases to be taken to court, seeking compensation from the Government for the physical, sexual, and emotional abuse they said was inflicted by senior pupils and staff. Their accounts were "remarkably consistent", Ms Cooper said.

She had also been contacted by a woman and her mother who used to live near Campbell Park, saying they had witnessed some of the bullying. They were willing to make statements in court. "What we're discovering as we're hearing more and more stories is that those in care institutions, including foster placements, had a very high likelihood of abuse - physical, sexual, or emotional."

Ms Cooper has become known for her work with abuse victims, handling cases from former patients at Porirua Hospital and various Department of Social Welfare institutions. Meanwhile, a former pupil said Campbell Park School in the 1930s and 40s was a cruel place but the pupils also had fun. The man said he saw no sexual abuse at the school while he was there from 1936 to 1945.

- NZPA

Celebrating Our Past. Building Our Future. P..

Oamaru

MONDAY AUGUST 4 2014 | OAMARU MAIL 3

Campbell Park old boy
hopes to turn book into film

By Ruby Harfield

RAISING FUNDS: Former Campbell Park Special School student Darryl Smith hopes to turn his book into a film.
PHOTO: SUPPLIED

Proudly Local Since 1876.

Mail

$25,000 is need to make the movie. If you finish the more than 5% less $125,000 we can talk about that.

027 483 - 1906

COOPER LEGEL LETTERS

COOPER LEGAL
Barristers and Solicitors

Level 1
Gleneagles Building
69-71 The Terrace
Wellington
PO Box 10899
The Terrace, Wellington 6143
Telephone: 04-4999025
Fax: 04-4999099
Email:sonjac@cooperlegal.co.nz
www.cooperlegal.co.nz

S M Cooper
23 May 2012

Darryl Smith
Flat 3
145 Princes Street
Strathurn
Invercargill
SOUTHLAND 9812

Dear Darryl

DEPARTMENT OF SOCIAL WELFARE CLAIM

Thank you for your telephone call into the office on 18 May 2012.

We are now writing to pass onto you, what we hope will be good news.

On 23 May 2012, we received an offer from Crown Law on behalf of the Ministry of Social Development, to settle your claim.

The offer is as follows:

- A settlement payment to you of $30,000, in acknowledgement of the likely abuse you suffered while in the custody of the Department of Social Welfare;
- Payment of your legal costs, as fixed by Legal Aid, so that you keep the full $30,000 for your personal use;
- An additional payment of $3,000 to support your work as an artist and in recognition that your artwork has been of great therapeutic value;
- A letter to you for the Chief Executive of MSD acknowledging and apologising for the Department's failings; and
- An offer to assist you to access suitable counselling services (whether through ACC or another provider), if you wish.

In addition, Garth Young from MSD has offered to arrange for you to travel to Wellington to receive the letter of apology, in person.

In terms of making the settlement offer, MSD accepts as follows:

Campbell Park School

MSD accepts that you were sexually abused by Campbell Park staff member, Mr Mathers. This is because of your consistency and credibility and also because Mr Mathers had a subsequent conviction for sexual offending.

MSD also accepts that you were physically abused by staff members Mr Mathers, Mr Shakespeare and Mr Parsons. As well as the physical abuse, MSD accepts that you were emotionally and verbally abused by staff at Campbell Park, including Mr Mathers, Mr Parsons and Mr Johnson.

As well as the above, MSD is prepared to accept that you were sexually abused by other residents and were involved in sexual activity with other residents. MSD acknowledges that it did not do enough to actively protect you, knowing you were a target for bullies during both admissions to Campbell Park. Further, MSD accepts that you were physically and emotionally bullied at Campbell Park by residents and by staff members, including Mr Mathers, Mr Shakespeare, Mr Johnson and Mr Parsons.

Finally, in terms of Campbell Park, MSD accepts that staff failed to either protect you (knowing your vulnerability), supervise adequately, or take appropriate action knowing you were the victim of bullying.

Christchurch Boys' Home (Stanmore Road)

MSD accepts it is more likely than not that you were physically abused by Mr Shakespeare at Stanmore Road. This is based on Mr Shakespeare's treatment of you while you were at Campbell Park.

MSD also accepts that you were sexually abused by at least one other resident at Stanmore Road. However, MSDs assessment is that staff at Stanmore Road were aware of the potential risks faced by you and demanded that a more suitable placement be found for you. Ultimately, you were returned to Stanmore Road as there were no other placements available and MSDs position is that monitoring was put in place to check your safety.

MSD does not accept that you spent a month in secure at Stanmore. While there is a record of you being sent to secure for three hours, there is no reference to you spending a lengthy period of time there.

Educational and life skills development

MSD does not accept it failed to provide you with an adequate education or life skills. It states that placement at Campbell Park was appropriate for you and the records show that you were given an individual programme and showed improvement.

Other allegations

As to the remaining allegations, MSD is unable to conclude you were physically, sexually or emotionally/mentally assaulted in the manner you described in your statement of claim, at Tahunanui and Moray Family Homes.

Summary

MSD has stated that it acknowledges the very positive engagement through this process it has had with you and wants to bring matters to a conclusion for you so that you can continue to move forward in your life.

Our advice to you is that you should consider accepting the offer. While there are aspects of your claim that have not been accepted, in the main MSD has accepted your description of life for you in Social Welfare care.

Comparing this offer with other offers made to clients who had similar experiences to you, we can reassure you that this is completely in line with those offers.

We are happy to discuss this with you, but if you accept our advice that you should accept this offer, then we would be grateful to receive your letter, in writing, instructing us to accept the offer and also giving us instructions as to how we should deal with the settlement funds.

Darryl, we realise this has been a long process for you. Nevertheless, we are now getting close to an end and we are glad we have finally reached this position for you. We now look forward to hearing from you in relation to the offer.

Yours sincerely

Sonja M Cooper
Principal

MESSAGE FROM BRENDON BOYLE CEO OF MINISTRY OF SOCIAL DEVELOPMENT

Message from Brendan - One year on
01 October 2012.

Hi everyone,

Today is a very special day for me as it marks the end of my first year as Chief Executive. Looking back, it's been a huge 12 months.

I'd have to say that the first couple of months went by in a bit of a blur, and shortly after the general election, the Government embarked on one of the most significant programmes of work for the whole of the Public Service. They've tasked us with a number of big ticket programmes - Welfare Reform, developing the Green and White Papers for vulnerable Children, investing in services for outcomes and tackling benefit fraud. It's been busy and these programmes have an impact on how we do our work, right across the Ministry, and I appreciate that a lot have been asked of us. I've seen up close the hard graft that you've put in, and your desire to give your very best and we have delivered.

While these areas of work have presented challenges and kept me focussed, it is the people of this Ministry that have made the greatest impact on me. When I started, I committed to getting out and talking with as many of you as possible. Looking back, I feel like I've been living the words of that song "I've been everywhere, man!" In the last twelve months, I've had the privilege of visiting every one of the Ministry's regions. This time last year I started with a visit to the top of the North, flying up to Kaitaia and since that time I've been to some of our offices at the bottom of the South Island, and almost everywhere in between. Just last week, I was in Hamilton with the Leadership Team at a Staff Engagement Forum.

No matter where I've visited and who I've met, I have always walked away with the same impression. I am in awe of the fantastic job that you do every day to help our most vulnerable New Zealanders. Getting to know you all a little better has been a truly humbling experience.

As I look ahead to the next twelve months, the challenges have in no way diminished. We are a big organisation and with that comes a great deal of responsibility. More and more it's clear that we can only hope to produce lasting, meaningful outcomes with the support of our partners. When we work across agencies, with NGOs and with individuals, we must always be conscious of how we are perceived. We need to stay grounded, walk alongside wherever possible and encourage all the way.

When I came into this job I knew about this Ministry's great reputation to deliver. What the last year has taught me is that I now know for certain that we're up for the challenge. I'm proud to say that I'm the Chief Executive of the Ministry of Social Development and I'd like to extend my personal thanks for all the support and encouragement from staff from right across the Ministry. Thanks for helping make this first year a great one.

Cheers,

Brendan

CONFIDENTIAL LISTENING AND ASSISTANCE SERVICE LETTERS AND MORE

Confidential Listening and Assistance Service
Ratonga Matatapu mō te Rongo me te Awhina

20 August 2010

Darryl Smith
6/31 Worcester Street
CHRISTCHURCH 8013

Dear Darryl

Further to my telephone conversation with you today, I have enclosed an authority for you to sign and return to me in the pre-paid envelope. Once I receive this signed authority back from you, I will then make a formal referral for you to the Ministry of Education. They will then be in touch with you to arrange an appointment to discuss your concerns.

As you are currently legally represented by Sonja Cooper, there are protocols that have to be cleared before the Ministry of Education is able to meet with you. They are happy to meet with you, with or without your lawyer present, but you will need to speak to Sonja Cooper about this first.

Are you able to contact your lawyer, Darryl and ask her to email Jan Breakwell of the Ministry of Education to clear the way for the meeting to proceed. They are not able to further this request until they have had some communication from your lawyer.

With regard to visiting Campbell Park, the Ministry of Education have no problem in principle with you and the Confidential Listening and Assistance Service visiting the school. However, it is dependent on the ownership of the property and gaining their permission.

I look forward to receiving the signed authority and hearing from you in due course.

Kind regards

Shelley Gabrielle
FACILITATOR

PO Box 5009, Lambton Quay, Wellington 6145 •
Email: info@listening.govt.nz • Phone 0800 268 587
Administered by The Department of Internal Affairs Te Tari Taiwhenua

Confidential Listening and Assistance Service
Ratonga Matatapu mō te Rongo me te Āwhina

14 September 2009

Mr Darryl Smith
33 Kana Street
MATAURA 9712

Dear Mr Smith

Thank you for your phone call to the Confidential Listening and Assistance Service. We note that you are interested in attending a Panel Meeting with the Service.

Talking with the panel will provide an opportunity for you to talk about past concerns and help identify your current needs for support and assistance. Claire Booth will be the Facilitater responsible for supporting you through the process. Claire will be in touch with you at a later date to let you know when the Panel will be in your area. In the meantime if you have any queries you can contact Claire on 0800 356 567.

I have enclosed our pamphlet and a copy of *Frequently Asked Questions* for your information.

Once again thank you for your call and we will be in touch with you again shortly.

Yours sincerely

Gordon McFedyen
EXECUTIVE OFFICER

PO Box 5939, Lambton Quay, Wellington 6145 •
Email: info@listening.govt.nz • Phone 0800 356 567
Administered by The Department of Internal Affairs Te Tari Taiwhenua

It will then be your opportunity to talk about your concerns and your experiences. The Panel may ask questions to check they understand or to clarify something. Sometimes the Panel may suggest a short break during the meeting and you can also ask for a break if you wish to.

What you tell the Panel will be confidential (unless you tell the Panel that you are very worried about hurting yourself or someone else). Any information you give will not be made public.

Tikanga Maori
If you would like a Kaumatua or Kuia on the panel or supporting you please let me know. If you wish to speak to the Panel in Te Reo please let me know and I can arrange an interpreter. Likewise, if you wish to speak in another language, please let me know.

Preparing for the Meeting
If you would like some help to work out how you would best like to present your concerns to the Panel, and to prepare for the meeting I will be happy to assist you.

Transport
Please discuss any transport difficulties with me so that your needs can be addressed. In some instances it may be possible to refund travel costs to attend the meeting.

Recording the Meeting
If you wish your meeting to be recorded please let the Panel know on the day of the meeting. The recording will be treated as confidential and you will be given a copy on CD. The service will keep a copy of the recording on a secure database but this will be destroyed at a future date.

Documents/Records
You are welcome to bring any documents or records with you that will help you give your account.

After the Meeting
After the meeting you are welcome to go return to the private waiting room for some light refreshments until you feel ready to leave. I will be available during this time to talk with you about any follow up assistance that has been agreed by the Panel.

If you need any special assistance for the meeting or have any questions, please telephone me 0800 356 567.

Yours sincerely

Shelley Gabrielle
FACILITATOR

Confidential Listening and Assistance Service
Ratonga Matatapu mō te Rongo me te Āwhina

SHOULD YOU REQUIRE SUPPORT AFTER YOUR MEETING

Thank you for coming today and telling the Panel of your experiences and concerns.

Friends and Family
Even if you do not wish to discuss anything about your meeting with the Panel, friends and family will be especially helpful to you at this time.

Other avenues of Support
Other useful people/organisations to contact if you feel you would like support after meeting with the Panel are:

- Your general practitioner

- Your community support worker

- *Lifeline:* ph 0800 543-354 (24 hour telephone counselling). Lifelines aim is to support and encourage people in uncovering new hope and steps towards finding a way through problems.

- *Samaritans:* ph 0800 726 666 (anytime day or night). For people who want confidential listening and support.

In an emergency please contact your local Community Assessment and Treatment Team (CATT):

Adult Community Mental Health Service – Psychiatric Emergency Service:
Phone: 0800 920-092 or 364-0482
Address: 74 Oxford Terrace, Christchurch

Lifeline Christchurch
Phone: 0800 543-354 or 366-6743
Website: www.lifeline.co.nz/chch/

PO Box 5806, Lambton Quay, Wellington 6145 •
Email: info@listening.govt.nz • Phone 0800 356 567
Administered by The Department of Internal Affairs Te Tari Taiwhenua

Confidential Listening and Assistance Service

Frequently Asked Questions

What is the Confidential Listening and Assistance Service?
The Confidential Listening and Assistance Service (the Service) is a body established by the Government to listen to the experiences of and to provide assistance to those who allege abuse or neglect or have concerns about their time in State care. People who are being invited to attend will include those who have lived in psychiatric hospitals and wards, health camps, child welfare care and special education homes before 1992.

Why has the Service been established?
The Service is largely based on the Confidential Forum for Former In-Patients of Psychiatric Hospitals, established in 2004, to provide an opportunity for former in-patients to speak about their experiences. Given the success of Confidential Forum, the Government decided to extend the listening and assistance services of the forum to all those in State care in psychiatric hospitals and wards, health camps, child welfare care and special education homes before 1992 rather than just those who were in psychiatric hospitals.

When was the Service established and how long will it run for?
The Service was established in late 2008 and is calling for expressions of interest from people who wish to tell of their experiences and concerns to the panel. You can contact the Service now on Phone 0800 356 987, by email info@listening.govt.nz or by writing to PO Box 5909, Lambton Quay, Wellington 6145. It is anticipated that the Service will run for a period of approximately five years. However, this length of time depends on the number of participants who choose to take part in the Service. The Service may operate for a lesser or greater period of time depending on demand.

Who is eligible to participate in the Service?
The Service is open to those who have lived in psychiatric hospitals and wards, health camps, child welfare care and special education homes before 1992 and who wish to talk about their concerns and/or experiences. If participants wish, their families/whanau or support people may attend to support them.

Why is the Service only open to those who were in State care before 1992?
This date was considered relevant because it reflects the time by which these sectors had modernised their standards and improved mechanisms to manage complaints.

What are the functions of the Service?
The functions of the Service are

- to provide the opportunity for participants to talk about their concerns and/or experiences with a panel of suitably qualified people.
- to help participants identify their current needs and get assistance to access services.
- to enable participants to access information held about them by the State, so they can ask questions and seek correction to any of that information.
- to assist participants to come to terms with their experience as far as it is reasonable.

The Service is not intended to determine liability or make judgements about the truth of participants' experiences or stories, nor recommend the payment of compensation.

2

How does the Service operate?

The Service supports a panel of appropriately qualified individuals who meet with participants and hear of their experiences and concerns. Members of the panel are selected because they are familiar with State care in New Zealand, and have a significant and respected community profile.

The panel listens and suggests ways of getting help, but it cannot make judgements about the truth of what it hears, or acknowledge liability for what happened, or directly resolve differences. The panel cannot order payment of compensation. Appearing at a panel hearing does not affect a participant's rights to take legal action.

Talking with the panel will provide an opportunity for participants to talk about past concerns and help identify current needs for support and assistance.
Where needed, counselling will be available for those who take part in the meetings.

Participants will be heard in a comfortable, confidential and private setting. The panel is normally made up of three members but meetings can be held with two members if necessary. Participants may also be permitted to have their story heard by one member alone if this is what they would prefer.

A Facilitator is available to participants to provide them with support and advice through the process of the panel meeting and implement assistance.

What sort of assistance can the Service provide?

Talking with the panel will provide an opportunity for participants to reflect on the past and look to the future with a focus on their current needs.

Assessment and, where needed, counselling will be available for those who participate in the meetings. The panel will assist participants to identify their needs, and gain access to services.

If required the panel will enable participants to access information held about them by the State, in an environment where they can ask questions and seek correction to the information held.

Why has Judge Henwood been chosen to chair the Service?

Judge Carolyn Henwood has been appointed Chair of the Service. Judge Henwood is a member of the New Zealand Parole Board and has over 20 years experience as a District Court and Youth Court Judge. During that time, Judge Henwood has been involved with youth and criminal justice issues, as well as having significant involvement in the arts. Judge Henwood has also been involved in Te Hurihanga, a residential programme aimed at preventing youth re-offending. The mediation and negotiation skills that Judge Henwood has developed throughout her career will be of great assistance to help participants talk about their concerns or experience in State care.

Who are the panel members?

Judge Henwood chairs a panel of three to listen to the stories of those who allege abuse and neglect while in state care. Panel members have been appointed on the basis of their expertise and standing in the community. The pool of panel members available to assist the Chair are: Paula Daye, Dr Barbara Disley, Dr Ian Hassall, Mike Noonan, Mata Hamani, and Areta Koopu.

What will happen at the panel meeting?

The Chair will welcome participants, introduce the panel to participants and support people. The Chair will offer the participant an opportunity for karakia or other relevant protocol to open the meeting. After the Chair has opened with some introductory remarks, the participant is then given an opportunity to talk about their experience in state care and to identify the key messages that

4

Can I have a record of my meeting with the panel?
Participants are able to record their session with the panel if they so
desire. A digital recorder will be available at the panel meeting and a recording of the proceedings
can be provided should a participant request it.

Can I bring somebody to support me at the meeting with the panel?
Participants may have up to two support people (but not legal representatives) at a time with them
in the panel meeting. Support people will not have speaking rights except with the permission of
the panel. The Chair may agree to allow more support people to accompany the participant to the
panel meeting if it is appropriate.

Will the Service impact on litigation that is already before the Courts?
Litigation will be able to continue separately from the work of the Service – no participant's rights
are affected by attendance at the hearing. The work of the Service is not to confirm truth or guilt
but is designed to assist people with their present practical and emotional needs arising from their
experiences in State care.

If I participated in the Confidential Forum can I also participate in the Service?
The Terms of Reference do not explicitly exclude this possibility. It will be up to the Service if it
allows those who have previously participated in the Confidential Forum to also participate in the
Service.

Who is responsible for administering the Service?
The Department of Internal Affairs will have responsibility for appointing the panel members and
administering the Service. The Service operates as an independent entity.

WEBSITE:
www.listening.govt.nz

COPPER LEGAL NEWSLETTERS

Sonja M. Cooper LL.B (Hons), B.A.

BARRISTER & SOLICITOR

PO Box 10899
The Terrace
Wellington
Telephone : 04 499 9025
Fax : 04 499 0299
Email: sonja@smcooperlaw.co.nz

DEPARTMENT OF SOCIAL WELFARE ACTION NEWSLETTER
First quarter 2006

Update

Inquiries are still coming in from persons who were in Department of Social Welfare care, whether in State-run institutions or foster care during the period 1960-2000. We have now prepared a data-base, which we are using to identify the numbers of clients who were in particular institutions and particular abuses who worked or those institutions. We have prepared the first large group of claims to be filed in Court. We have delayed filing these claims for reasons to be explained in this newsletter, but they are being prepared for filing soon.

Interviews and records

Regular trips are made out of the office and around New Zealand to interview clients in this group. All staff, including myself, continue to take trips to interview clients. Please make sure you attend interviews at the time and place we have set with you. Again, please note we are funded generally for one interview only. It is important we come so much information with you in that interview as possible.

We continue to have lengthy delays in receiving records, particularly from CYFS. In some cases, now, we have been waiting for over a year. Please understand that we are unable to advance your claim until we have your records. In addition to CYFS records, we are also obtaining your Corrections and Ministry of Justice records. If you have been receiving ACC, we will be obtaining those records as well. When we are ready to advance your claim in Court, we will ask you to sign specific authority documents so that we can track down records from WINZ, IRD and Archives (for school records).

Expert Reports

Unless we reach further agreement with Crown Law, it will be necessary at some stage for each one of you to be seen by a psychiatrist to assess you and provide a report for us about why it has taken you until the present time to bring your claim and also identify what damage you have suffered as a result of Social Welfare care. As stated in previous newsletters, it is important that you co-operate with the report writer when we set up an interview. We have only a few psychiatrists to work with and their time is precious.

Media

We continue to be reluctant to run a story in the media about the claims. New clients continue to come into the office, referred from a number of sources, including counsellors. We still need to make significant inroads into care work, before the media run with the story again. We are working hard to progress the claims during the course of this year.

Other claims

We continue to have clients who we are helping to bring claims against churches including the Salvation Army, the Catholic Church, the Anglican Church, and so on. As stated, many churches (in religious orders) are developing procedures for dealing with claims against them. We will let you know what the process will be for your particular claim.

Change of contact details

We request you to let us know if you change address and/or telephone number. It is important that we can, at all times, contact you.

Prioritisation of work

For various legal and practice reasons we are giving priority to certain claims. In particular, we are working to progress claims for those clients who are under the age of 20, or were not in a DSW institution, but in foster care/family unit; and/or instituted in in 2005/6. If you are part of this group and have not heard from us within the next three months, please contact us to see what progress we are making.

Crown Law / Department of Child Youth and Family

In January 2006, we delivered a paper to Crown Law and the lawyers for CYFS, setting out in detail the allegations of abuse made by our clients who were in institutions run by DSW between the 1960s and 2000. That paper numbered just about of 200 pages. It shows how many of our clients identify particular staff abusers. It also provides detailed information of the 'culture' of abuse that pervaded each individual institution. This is a very important document. It has been prepared by us analysing each individual client's file and extracting information to form the larger document. CYFS will now use the document to undertake its own investigation. We have been advised that the document is important in that it will be used to inform the Government about the sorts of litigation. We are hopeful it may provide the basis, some time further down the track, for an 'out of Court' process to resolve your claims. We will keep you advised. We note that a burglar broke into the office over the Christmas break, taking all our laptops. The information used to draft the document was on one of the stolen laptops. The laptops have now been recovered, however, we have been advised that the perpetrator was a professional burglar and would have deleted the hard drive.

Test Case

Two of our clients' cases which were commenced some years ago will be heard either later this year or early next year. The clients (brothers) were under DSW care. They were in Hokio and Epuni. The cases are important in that they will test, for the first time, the liability of the Crown for young persons who suffered abuse in institutional care. We have contacted three of our clients who were in those institutions at the same time. We are keen to build up as strong a case as possible to demonstrate what it was like for young people living in DSW care. We will keep you advised on progress of this important case.

Joint DSW / Psychiatric Hospital Claims

We have been waiting for a decision from the High Court since July 2005, that will influence the way these claims must be brought. We have been told the decision will be delivered soon. We will have a separate newsletter when we can give more information about these cases.

Legal Aid

In our last two newsletters we explained what documentation is required for a grant of legal aid to be made. The Agency is requiring that, for all clients for whom we have been acting over two years, we update your financial details. Also, because we need to keep obtaining your records, it is important that we have an updated authority document. For that reason, we are enclosing a new legal aid form and authority document to complete. For those of you who have not completed the relevant forms, we are enclosing those documents as well. In some cases, we will be providing you with a stamped, self-addressed envelope to return those documents into the office as soon as possible. Without the proper documentation, we cannot continue with our work.

Contact with this firm

It is important for you to know that Olive, our secretary/receptionist, has been in hospital – having suffered a critical illness. Sam is filling in. This means there will be delays with some work, however we are doing our best. Once again, we remind you not to make unexpected visits to the office. We are very busy and mostly do not have time to fit in unexpected visitors. We also do our best to return phone calls, however please note that we do not generally accept collect calls except by prior arrangement. The team continues to grow. At present, we comprise Sonja, Sarah, Ruth, Karyn, Amanda, Bronwyn, Anne and Sam.

Sonja M Cooper

PLEASE NOTE: If you have any questions about this newsletter or the attached forms please contact Sam at the office.

Sonja M. Cooper LLB (Hons), BA

BARRISTER & SOLICITOR

PO Box 10899
The Terrace
Wellington

Telephone   04-499 9025
Fax   04-499 9299

DEPARTMENT OF SOCIAL WELFARE ACTION

March 2004

This newsletter is designed so that I can spend less time writing out letters to you and more time working on your case. Please accept the important aspect of it, I have however in excess of 100 ex-Department of Social Welfare clients now seeking to joining a claim. I will only use the newsletter to make general announcements. I will deal with you for all personal matters.

Update

To date, I have received enquiries from about 200 persons who were in Department of Social Welfare care (whether in state run institutions or foster care) during the period 1960-1992.

For all of these persons, we have sent out a bundle of information including the law dealing with historic abuse claims; information about funding of the claims; and recent newspaper articles.

A good number of those to whom we have written have already returned the documentation we require to get funding organised. Many have not yet done that and it is important that this is actioned as quickly as possible.

To be done

The next steps that need to be taken are:

- Receiving outstanding legal aid applications and processing the applications for legal aid.
- Obtaining new records from the Child Youth and Family Service.
- Organising interviews to interview you individually.
- Arranging for experts to attend on some of you in order to prepare expert reports.

From previous experience, this step is time-consuming. We are still processing about 2 new enquiries per day from clients who are keen to join the group. We intend to take on an extra staff member who will responsible for the administrative handling of this aspect of the claim.

Contacting others

A number of the clients contacted by our firm have been keen to get in touch with others who were in Social Welfare care at the same time as them. Ethical and legal constraints prevent us from making available our client lists. Nevertheless, we have already been able to put some clients in touch with other clients who have consented to their information being shared.

Some of our clients have also helpfully set up website pages to enable members of the group who are interested in doing so, to communicate with one another. This website details are:

- www.oldfriends.co.nz Your last name and name of institution

Media Interests

We are keen to get interested in stories from people who had

abusive experiences in Social Welfare care. We are aware that there has been a lot of media interest at Campbell Park School, in South Island newspapers and on the radio. We are also aware of media interest at what happened in institutions such as Pareheni House (Wairarapa) and the lower North Island institutions including Kohitere, Holate Beach and Epuni Boys' Home.

If any of you would like to tell your story to the media in the future, would you please indicate that to us so that we can keep a record of that on your file. It is important that we keep the media interested in this story so that we can put pressure on the Government to set up a public enquiry when we are ready for that.

If you are in receipt of a grant of legal aid:

There are two forms attached to this newsletter. We would like you to write in your name on the form, date the form, and sign it. The form is a consent to share certain costs.

The reason we can progress your claim on its substantial basis is that there is a very large group of you complaining about the same, or very similar things. Court proceedings ordinarily cost a considerable amount of money. There are certain steps involved in bringing a claim that the group as a whole will benefit from. These are things like, filing fees, expert bills, and disbursements. By signing the form, you are agreeing to these costs being spread among you. If you work together as a group, we can reduce the cost of our work and thereby minimise what you need to gain from the Court proceedings.

The second item we complete is for those who have legal aid or are applying for legal aid. Because of the expertise that I have in bringing these types of claims, the Legal Services Agency has agreed a special hourly rate to other this. The hourly rate is $200 per hour, excluding GST. This hourly rate, while more than normal legal aid rates, is still over 150 less than my usual hourly rate. The Legal Services Agency has said that this arrangement needs your consent and so I attach a consent which I would ask that you sign and return with the other documents.

Contact with this firm

Please feel free to get in touch with us if you have any issues or questions about what we are doing or about your particular case. The person who will be most familiar with all of the files is Carla Leader and she should be your first point of contact. Carla and I are our usually discussing the clients generally, as well as those individual file so I am always up to date with what is happening. Because of my other work commitments, however, I am not as easy to get hold of.

Or, in general terms, it has been only really while we have contact with so many of you over the last few months. We do feel this is an important and notified process and we are committed to seeing this through to a proper outcome.

Sonja M Cooper
Carla L Leader

'Sonja M. Cooper LL.B (Hons) B.A
BARRISTER & SOLICITOR

P.O. Box 10289
The Terrace
Wellington

Telephone   : 04-499 9025
Fax   : 04-499 0299

DEPARTMENT OF SOCIAL WELFARE ACTION
March 2004

This newsletter is designed so that I can spend less time writing out letters to you and more time working on your case. Please excuse the impersonal aspect of it. I have however in excess of 100 ex-Department of Social Welfare clients now seeking to bring a claim. I will only use the newsletter to make general announcements. I will deal with you for all personal matters.

Update

To date, I have received enquiries from about 200 persons who were in Department of Social Welfare care (whether in state run institutions or foster care) during the period 1960-1980.

For all of those persons, we have sent out a bundle of information including, the law dealing with historic abuse claims; information about funding of the claims; and recent newspaper articles.

A good number of those to whom we have written have already returned the documentation we require to get funding organised. Many have not yet done that and it is important that this is actioned as quickly as possible.

To be done

The next steps that need to be taken are:

- Receiving outstanding legal aid application and processing the applications for legal aid.
- Obtaining your records from the Child Youth and Family Service.
- Organising interviewers to interview you individually.
- Arranging for experts to attend on some of you in order to prepare expert reports.

From previous experience, this step is time-consuming. We are still processing about 2 new enquiries per day from clients who are keen to join the group. We intend to take on an extra staff member who will responsible for the administrative handling of this aspect of the claim.

Contacting others

A number of the clients contacted by our firm have been keen to get in touch with others who were in Social Welfare care at the same time as them. Ethical and legal constraints prevent us from making available our client lists. Nevertheless, we have already been able to put some clients in touch with other clients who have consented to their information being shared.

Some of our clients have also helpfully set up website pages to enable members of the group who are interested in doing so, to communicate with one another. Those website details are:

- www.oldfriends.co.nz (then link to city and name of institution)

Media Interest

The media are very interested in stories from people who had abusive experiences in Social Welfare care. We are aware that there has been a lot of media interest in Campbell Park School, in South Island newspapers and on the radio. We are also aware of media interest in what happened in institutions such as Fareham House (Wairarapa) and the lower North Island institutions including Kohitere, Hokio Beach and Epuni Boys' Home.

If any of you would like to tell your story to the media in the future, would you please indicate that to us so that we can keep a record of that on your file. It is important that we keep the media interested in this story so that we can put pressure on the Government to set up a public enquiry where we are ready for that.

If you are in receipt of a grant of legal aid:

There are two forms attached to this newsletter. We would like you to state in your name on the front, date the form, and sign it. The form is a consent to share certain costs.

The reason we can progress your claim on an economical basis is that there is a very large group of you complaining about the same, or very similar things. Court proceedings ordinarily cost a considerable amount of money. There are certain costs involved in bringing a claim that the group as a whole will benefit from. Those are things like, filing fees, expert bills, and disbursements. By signing the form, you are agreeing to these costs being spread among you. If you work together as a group, we can reduce the cost of our work and thereby maximise what you stand to gain from the Court proceedings.

The second form to complete is for those who have legal aid or are applying for legal aid. Because of the expertise that I have in bringing these types of claims, the Legal Services Agency has agreed a special hourly rate to reflect this. The hourly rate is $200 per hour, including GST. This hourly rate, while more than normal legal aid rates, is still over $50 less than my usual hourly rate. The Legal Services Agency has said that this arrangement needs your consent and so I attach a consent which I would ask that you sign and return with the other documents.

Contact with this firm

Please feel free to get in touch with us if you have any issues or questions about what we are doing or about your particular case. The person who will be most familiar with all of the files is Carla Leader and she should be your first point of contact. Carla and I are constantly discussing the claims generally, as well as each individual file so I am always up to date with what is happening. Because of my other work commitments, however, I am not as easy to get hold of.

On a general note, it has been really worth while to have contact with so many of you over the last few months. We do feel this is an important and justified process and we are committed to seeing this through to a proper outcome.

Sonja M Cooper
Carla L Leader

PLEASE NOTE: If you have any questions about this newsletter or the attached forms please contact Carla Leader at the office, details above. If you have access to email I recommend that you contact her on carla@smcooperlaw.co.nz

`Sonja M. Cooper

BARRISTER & SOLICITOR

PO Box 10899
The Terrace
Wellington

Telephone : 04-499 9025
Fax : 04-499 9276

DEPARTMENT OF SOCIAL WELFARE ACTION
March 2004

This newsletter is designed so that I can spend less time writing out letters to you and more time working on your case. Please excuse the impersonal aspect of it. I have however in excess of 100 ex-Department of Social Welfare clients now seeking to bring a claim. I will only use the newsletter to make general announcements. I will deal with you for all personal matters.

Update

To date, I have received enquiries from about 200 persons who were in Department of Social Welfare care (whether in state run institutions or foster care) during the period 1960-1990.

For all of those persons, we have sent out a bundle of information including: the law dealing with historic abuse claims; information about funding of the claims; and recent newspaper articles.

A good number of those in whom we have written have already returned the documentation we require to get funding approved. Many have not yet done that and it is important that this is actioned as quickly as possible.

To be done

The next steps that need to be taken are:

- Receiving outstanding legal aid applications and processing the applications for legal aid.
- Obtaining your records from the Child Youth and Family Service.
- Organising interviewers to interview you individually.
- Arranging for experts to attend on some of you in order to prepare expert reports.

From previous experience, this step is time-consuming. We are still processing about 2 new enquiries per day from clients who are keen to join the group. We intend to take on an extra staff member who will responsible for the administrative handling of this aspect of the claim.

Contacting others

A number of the clients contacted by our firm have been keen to get in touch with others who were in Social Welfare care at the same time as them. Ethical and legal constraints prevent us from making available our client lists. Nevertheless, we have already been able to put some clients in touch with other clients who have consented to their information being shared.

Some of our clients have also helpfully set up website pages to enable members of the group who are interested in doing so, to communicate with one another. Those website details are:

- www.oldfriends.co.nz (then link to city and name of institution)

Media Interest

The media are very interested in stories from people who had abusive experiences in Social Welfare care. We are aware that there has been a lot of media interest in Campbell Park School, in South Island newspapers and on the radio. We are also aware of media interest in what happened in institutions such as Fareham House (Wanganui) and the lower North Island institutions including Kohitere, Hokio Beach and Epuni Boys' Home.

If any of you would like to tell your story to the media in the future, would you please indicate that to us so that we can keep a record of that on your file. It is important that we keep the media interested in this story so that we can put pressure on the Government to set up a public enquiry when we are ready for that.

If you are in receipt of a grant of legal aid

There are two forms attached to this newsletter. We would like you to write in your name on the form, then the form, and sign it. The form is a consent to client certain costs.

The reason we can progress your claim on an economical basis is that there is a very large group of you complaining about the same, or very similar things. Court proceedings ordinarily cost a considerable amount of money. There are certain costs involved in bringing a claim that the group as a whole will benefit from. Those are things like, filing fees, expert bills, and disbursements. By signing the form, you are agreeing to these costs being spread among you. If you work together as a group, we can reduce the cost of our work and thereby minimise what you stand to pay from the Court proceedings.

The second form to complete is for those who have legal aid or are applying for legal aid. Because of the expertise that I have in bringing these types of claims, the Legal Services Agency has agreed a special hourly rate to reflect this. The hourly rate is $200 per hour, including GST. This hourly rate, while more than normal legal aid rates, is still over 5% less than my usual hourly rate. The Legal Services Agency has said that this arrangement needs your consent and so I attach a consent which I would ask that you sign and return with the other documents.

Contact with this firm

Please feel free to get in touch with us if you have any issues or questions about what we are doing or about your particular case. The person who will be most familiar with all of the files is Ceris Leader and she should be your first point of contact. Ceris and I are constantly discussing the claims generally, as well as each individual file so I am always up to date with what is happening. Because of my other work commitments, however, I am not so easy to get hold of.

On a general note, it has been really worth while to have contact with so many of you over the last few months. We do feel that it is an important and justified process and we are committed to seeing this through to a proper outcome.

Sonja M Cooper
Ceris L Leader

PLEASE NOTE if you have any questions about this newsletter or the attached forms please contact Ceris Leader at the office, details above. If you have access to email I recommend that you contact her on ceris@sonjacooper.co.nz

`Sonja M. Cooper` LL.B (Hons), BA.
BARRISTER & SOLICITOR

PO Box 10899
The Terrace
Wellington

Telephone : 04-499 8925
Fax : 04-499 0299

DEPARTMENT OF SOCIAL WELFARE ACTION
March 2004

This newsletter is designed so that I can spend less time writing our letters to you and more time working on your case. Please excuse the impersonal aspect of it. I have however in excess of 100 ex-Department of Social Welfare clients now seeking to bring a claim. I will only use the newsletter to make general announcements. I will deal with you for all personal matters.

Update

To date, I have received enquiries from about 280 persons who were in Departments of Social Welfare care (whether in state run institutions or foster care) during the period 1960-1990.

For all of these persons, we have sent out a bundle of information including the law dealing with historic abuse claims; information about funding of the claims; and recent newspaper articles.

A good number of those to whom we have written have already returned the documentation we require to get funding organised. Many have not yet done that and it is important that this is actioned as quickly as possible.

To be done

The next steps that need to be taken are:

- Receiving outstanding legal aid applications and processing the applications for legal aid.
- Obtaining your records from the Child Youth and Family Service.
- Organising interviews to interview you individually.
- Arranging for experts to attend on some of you in order to prepare expert reports.

From previous experience, this step is time-consuming. We are still processing about 2 new enquiries per day from clients who are keen to join the group. We intend to take on an extra staff member who will responsible for the administrative handling of this aspect of the claim.

Contacting others

A number of the clients contacted by our firm have been to get in touch with others who were in Social Welfare care at the same time as them. Ethical and legal constraints prevent us from making available our client lists. Nevertheless, we have already been able to put some clients in touch with other clients who have consented to their information being shared.

Some of our clients have also helpfully set up website pages to enable numbers of the group who are interested in doing so, to communicate with one another. These website details are:

- **www.oldfriends.co.nz** (then look in city and name of institution)

Media Interest

The media are very interested in stories from people who had abusive experiences in Social Welfare care. We are aware that there has been a lot of media interest in Campbell Park School, in South Island newspapers and on the radio. We are also aware of media interest in what happened in institutions such as Panther House (Whitianga) and the lower South Island institutions including Kohitere, Hokio Beach and Epuni Boys' Home.

If any of you would like to tell your story to the media in the forum, would you please indicate that to us so that we can keep a record of that on your file. It is important that we keep the media interested in this story so that we can put pressure on the Government to set up a public enquiry when we are ready for that.

If you are in receipt of a grant of legal aid:

There are two forms attached to this newsletter. We would like you to write in your name on the form, date the form, and sign it. The form is a consent to share certain costs.

The reason we can progress your claim on an economical basis is that there is a very large group of you complaining about the same, or very similar things. Court proceedings ordinarily cost a considerable amount of money. There are certain costs involved in bringing a claim that the group as a whole will benefit from. These are things like, filing fees, expert bills, and disbursements. By signing the form, you are agreeing to these costs being spread evenly out. If you work together as a group, we can reduce the cost of our work and thereby minimise what you stand to gain from the Court proceedings.

The second form to complete is for those who have legal aid or are applying for legal aid. Because of the expertise that I have in bringing these types of claims, the Legal Services Agency has agreed a special hourly rate to reflect this. The hourly rate is $200 per hour, including GST. This hourly rate, while more than normal legal aid rates, is still over $50 less than my usual hourly rate. The Legal Services Agency has said that this arrangement needs your consent and so I attach a consent which I would ask that you sign and return with the other documents.

Contact with this firm

Please feel free to get in touch with us if you have any issues or questions about what we are doing or about your particular case. The person who will be most familiar with all of the files is Carla Leader and she should be your first point of contact. Carla and I are constantly discussing the claim generally, as well as each individual file so I am always up to date with what is happening. Because of my other work commitments, however, I am not so easy to get hold of.

On a general note, it has been really worth while to have contact with so many of you over the last few months. We do feel this is an important and justified process and we are committed to seeing this through to a proper outcome.

Sonja M Cooper
Carla L Leader

PLEASE NOTE: If you have any questions about this newsletter or the attached forms please contact Carla Leader at the office, details above. If you have access to email I recommend that you contact her on carla@sonjacooper.co.nz.

COOPER LEGAL
Barristers and Solicitors

Level 1
Gleneagles Building
69-71 The Terrace
Wellington
PO Box 18999
The Terrace, Wellington, 6143
Telephone: 64-4699025
Fax: 04-4994299
Email: enquiries@cooperlegal.co.nz

PSYCHIATRIC HOSPITAL/DEPARTMENT OF SOCIAL WELFARE ACTION
3rd/4th Quarter 2010

Introduction:

It has been about 7 months since we last forwarded a newsletter regarding progress of the claims. We have been monitoring developments which affect your individual claims which will be addressed in this newsletter. We ask, therefore, that you read this newsletter carefully. We note that although you would usually receive both a Social Welfare and psychiatric hospital newsletter, the purpose of this single newsletter is to bring you up to date in respect of what has been happening with both groups.

Overview:

Since our last newsletters we have been:

• continuing to fight the LSA ("LSA") to maintain your funding, including arguing six appeals in the High Court. We have had some success;

• denied leave to appeal to the Supreme Court (New Zealand's highest court) in a Social Welfare case, to deal with important legal issues for historic abuse claimants, because of the difficult factual findings in that particular case;

• closing off the files of a small number of psychiatric hospital clients whose claims could not continue after the Supreme Court decision;

• starting to settle some individual Social Welfare claims (at this stage not many) through either direct negotiation with MSD, negotiations with Crown Law and MSD and/or through assistance from the High Court;

• developing a process by which some psychiatric hospital claims, at least, might be settled through the High Court; and

• continuing to maintain pressure on the Government and the Crown to settle the claims out of court, particularly through providing the Human Rights Commission with our input into its review of the Government's response to historic abuse claims.

Court action:

Psychiatric Hospital cases

We outlined the result of the Supreme Court decision in the psychiatric hospital cases in our previous newsletter. Regrettably, we have had to discontinue a small number of claims for clients where their allegations could not surmount the hurdles identified in our previous newsletter. We had hoped to work on every other client's case by amending the court documents to take into account the Supreme Court's decision. Although we asked the LSA for funding in April 2010, to do that work, we have not yet been advised that we can do it.

We did say that the High Court had allocated time in the middle of June 2011 for two psychiatric hospital cases to be heard. Because most of the psychiatric hospital cases are presently held up due to funding difficulties, we have had to advise the High Court that we cannot go ahead with the two cases. However, there has been a development in that regard which may mean some movement in the psychiatric hospital cases. That development is outlined below, in the section titled "Judicial Settlement Conferences".

Social Welfare cases

In our last newsletter, we advised you that we had appealed to the Court of Appeal against the decision of the Wellington High Court dealing with two brothers who were under DSW care. We received the Court of Appeal's decision on 23 April 2010. The decision went against our clients, mainly because of the findings of fact in respect of the Limitation Act issues for them, by the Judge in the High Court. As noted above, we did endeavour to appeal the Court of Appeal's decision to the Supreme Court, however we were refused leave. While the Supreme Court acknowledged that both brothers had undoubtedly undergone regrettable suffering during their childhood and adolescence, the Court held that the Limitation Act operated to stop them obtaining compensation.

We were very disappointed with the decisions from both the Court of Appeal and Supreme Court. We are now reviewing whether to take the brothers' claim to the United Nations, as that is our only option because we have exhausted all our options through the New Zealand courts.

As we said in the previous newsletter, two DSW cases were scheduled to go to trial in 2010. Another three cases were scheduled to go to trial in 2011. We have now settled the two cases scheduled for 2010, as well as two of the three cases scheduled for trial in 2011. The first case, in which our client was in Hamilton Boys' Home and Kohitere, was settled shortly before that trial was to start. By that stage, we had received documents about Kohitere and Hamilton Boys' Home. We had also received the statements of former staff members who, in the main, denied any wrongdoing. Having said that, some of the former Kohitere staff members did acknowledge that they "may have" assaulted boys and/or that they may have seen other staff members assault or otherwise mistreat boys. We hope that we may be able to settle the claims of other clients who were in Kohitere, in due course, in light of these helpful statements.

The second case we have settled involved foster care. The facts of that case related to the 1950s and to a particular foster home. We do not have any other clients who were in that foster home who might benefit from the outcome of that case, however it does show we can settle cases where there are limited witnesses.

Judicial Settlement Conferences

There has been an important new development that may lead to us being able to settle more cases. The High Court recently asked that we trial judicial settlement conferences ("JSCs") (conferences chaired by a High Court Judge whose job is to assist the parties to settle the claim), as a way of dealing with the very large number of claims before the High Court. This suggestion was made because of the High Court's observation that many of you **have** suffered harm as a result of your experiences in care and that you should receive some compensation for that. We have now trialled three Social Welfare clients' cases through the JSC process, including the foster home case referred to above, and have settled each of those cases. Only one of those cases involved a residence, in that case Campbell Park School (Otekaike). The other two cases involved abusive and/or neglectful parental and/or foster care.

We have already advised 5 other Social Welfare clients that their cases are set down for JSCs in 2011. Unfortunately we cannot progress the JSCs any quicker than that, as we have to do a large amount of preparation work, including receiving in all of the Department's documents about the client and the placements they resided at. We also have to

prepare statements on behalf of our clients, as well as witness statements and expert Limitation Act statements. In addition, the Crown has to prepare the same information, which we have to exchange well in advance of any JSC. We are hopeful, based on the success of the first 3 JSCs, that we may be able to start settling more DSW claims through this process. We will keep you advised, but warn that this is still a lengthy and time-consuming process.

We still have a number of DSW cases that are being contested by the Crown on the basis that clients are unable to get through the Limitation Act hurdle. As we stated in our last newsletter, in each of those cases we are required to provide to the Crown all relevant documents. We are then required to file written evidence setting out the reasons why the claim was not brought until it was. That invariably includes an expert report from a psychiatrist and/or psychologist.

For a number of DSW clients, this year, our psychiatric evidence has stated that the clients have brought their claims too late. For those clients, we have had no option but to discontinue their claims in the court. For the reasons we state later on in this newsletter, that will not necessarily be the end of matters for those clients, as we are hopeful there may yet be a process set up to deal with our clients' claims out of court.

We are hoping to trial some psychiatric hospital JSCs as soon as possible. It is likely that Johnston Lawrence, the other law firm we work with, will do the first one or two cases – given that we have been able to trial three Social Welfare cases already.

We are hopeful, based on the success of the Social Welfare JSCs, that we may be able to start settling some psychiatric hospital claims through this process. We will keep you advised, but warn that this will still be a lengthy and time-consuming process. Further, because we have not yet had any psychiatric hospital JSCs, we have no idea, at this point in time, what approach the Crown Health Financing Agency (and Crown Law) will have to settlement of the claims.

Legal aid:

We have referred to our problems with legal aid in the last few newsletters. Those problems are continuing. The LSA has withdrawn aid for a large number of our clients this year. In total, the LSA has withdrawn aid on over 56 psychiatric hospital files so far, which amounts to one-third of all psychiatric hospital client files managed by this firm. The LSA has also withdrawn aid for a large number of our DSW clients this year. In total, the LSA has withdrawn aid on over 80 DSW files so far.

As we advised in our last newsletter, for new clients whose applications were made up until December 2009, the LSA has refused to provide any funding at all to enable us to bring claims. We continue to challenge those decisions, by asking the Legal Aid Review Panel ("LARP") to review the LSA's decisions. Unfortunately, we have not yet had any decisions from LARP which may help in this area. We have also been told by the LSA that we should start receiving decisions about new clients within the next month or so. Those decisions will relate to all applications made since December 2009 (approximately 50 in total).

Since our last newsletter, we have argued six appeals brought by the LSA against LARP decisions which were favourable to our clients. The High Court heard two of those six appeals in March 2010 and issued its decisions in April 2010. On balance, the decisions have been helpful for us, although it is fair to say that we won one decision and lost the other. The problem is, however, with the Legal Services Agency, which tends to give limited effect to decisions which do not support its position.

We argued four further appeals from LARP in August 2010. We have no decision yet from the High Court. These appeals focused on what information we have to provide to the LSA, at the outset, in order to obtain legal aid for you. The decisions will be important ones and we await them with interest.

We have had increasing numbers of decisions from LARP this year in relation to the LSA's decisions withdrawing clients' legal aid. In the case of clients for whom we have not yet obtained a psychiatric report, most of the decisions have been favourable. In other words, LARP has reinstated legal aid to enable us to obtain an expert report which addresses Limitation Act issues. Unfortunately, we now have a big backlog of reports to obtain and only a very small number of experts who can do them. We apologise if you are one of the clients affected by that, however there is little we can do to speed up the process.

For those clients who do have expert reports, the outcome has not been so favourable. In more cases than not, to date, LARP has confirmed the LSA's decision to withdraw clients' legal aid. We consider that most of those decisions are wrong. We have, therefore, recommended to clients that we appeal LARP's decisions. We have already lodged 7 appeals and expect we will lodge more as the LARP decisions come through. It is unlikely that any of these appeals will be heard until next year.

We advised you in our last newsletter about the review of legal aid. The Government is now implementing a change whereby the LSA will be folded into the Ministry of Justice. We do have real concerns about what that will mean for the historic abuse claims, as your claims are against the Attorney-General. We will be making submissions to the Government about the need to ensure that your claims are dealt with fairly and with as much independence from Government as possible. We will keep you advised of developments.

We continue to have difficulties with the LSA in obtaining funding to undertake the work we need to do on your behalf. We are also having ongoing difficulties in having the LSA pay for work we have already undertaken for you. We did want to draw your attention, in particular, to the "global" invoices. The global invoices are the invoices we send in to the LSA every 3-4 months for work we have done **on behalf of the entire client group**. You will have received a number of letters from the LSA, recently, in respect of the global invoices. Please read those letters carefully, as they are confusing. Towards the top of the letter, you will be told what your share is of the global invoices, which will usually be a reasonably small amount (not exceeding a few hundred dollars). We do note that as the client group gets smaller because the LSA is withdrawing more and more clients' legal aid, the number of clients available to share the cost of the global bill also shrinks. Of course we are concerned about that and we are doing our best to keep work down as much as possible. Having said that, we still need to undertake work that is for the benefit of the entire client group, such as research, submissions to the United Nations and the Human Rights Commission, liaison with other lawyers and experts who work in this area and attendance at court and other conferences on your behalf.

As in previous newsletters, we encourage you to contact the LSA by telephone or letter, if you are unhappy about the LSA's decisions. We also understand that the LSA may have begun sending you out copies of all correspondence which it sends to this firm. A lot of that correspondence is incomprehensible and/or difficult to understand. While the Agency invites you to contact this firm, our suggestion is that you contact the LSA, as that will not incur cost on your file. The telephone number and contact address for the Agency will be on any correspondence you receive from it.

Please note: if we do not hear back from you promptly confirming that we should review any decision to withdraw your legal aid, or appeal a LARP decision upholding the withdrawal of your legal aid, or if we have no way to contact you, then we will not take any further steps on your file except to close it.

"Out of court" process:

Psychiatric Hospital cases

As in our last two newsletters, there have been no offers made by Crown Law to settle any psychiatric hospital claims. We continue to be extremely disappointed at this lack of progress. Having said that, we refer to the latest development discussed above, about the agreement to trial JSCs for psychiatric hospital clients. We can only "wait and see" if this results in settlements of your claims.

Social Welfare cases

As advised above, and in our previous newsletter, we are still receiving "one-off" offers to settle individual clients' claims. It is not always clear to us why MSD looks to settle one client's claims, but not others. We are hopeful that our progress over the course of this year in settling some claims will continue and that we will be able to settle more and more of our clients' claims. We remain of the vie that some cases will still need to go to trial to test the facts and/or the law.

We note our earlier advice that the offers we have had are at a very modest level, in other words just enough to be acceptable. Offers at the lower end have been under $10,000. Accordingly, you should have no expectation of a high settlement offer being made if we start on this process with you.

Our last letter referred to our contact with the Kapiti Police, who were investigating two former Epuni staff members in respect of several assault allegations. We advised that we had assisted the Police in providing information from our clients' files with our clients' consent and cooperation. We note one caution in that regard. The lawyer for one of the former Epuni staff members who has since been charged (and will shortly come to trial) has asked for disclosure of all information we hold on behalf of the clients involved in the trial, in respect of their time in Social Welfare care. We have had to provide that information, on a confidential basis, to the District Court Judge who is dealing with the trial. We have made strong submissions objecting to the disclosure of that material, on the grounds it was given to us in confidence. We are still awaiting

the outcome of that argument and will keep clients advised. This may happen in any future criminal trials of former staff members.

Care Claims & Resolution Team: *(Social Welfare cases)*

It continues to come to our attention that a number of clients have contacted, or have been contacted by, members of the Care Claims and Resolution Team run by MSD, which is the defendant in the DSW cases. As we stated in our last newsletter, it is very important that you discuss, with us, any contact that you have with that team – preferably before you do so. While we may not obtain funding to attend meetings with you, we certainly encourage you to involve us at the point at which MSD may look to settle your claim.

We make two points. First, you are liable to pay back any fees paid to this firm by the LSA out of any settlement funds you receive. We have, in the past, been able to negotiate with MSD so that they have paid a contribution to those costs, as part of any settlement arrangement. If we are not advised of the settlement of your claim and therefore do not have the opportunity to negotiation a contribution to your fees, the LSA will be able to simply "claw back" their repayment amount from the settlement funds.

Secondly, we have information from MSD that clearly shows clients who are represented by lawyers have better outcomes of settling, and for more, than those who do not have legal representation.

Human Rights Commission and United Nations:

You will be pleased to learn that the United Nations Committee Against Torture ("UNCAT") is still monitoring the New Zealand Government's handling of your claims. The Government provided a report to the UN in May 2010, which suggested that the claims were being handled appropriately. We replied to that report at the end of June 2010. We were strongly critical of the Government's report – pointing out numerous problems with the way in which the current approach to historic abuse claims is prejudicing our clients.

As stated above, the Human Rights Commission ("HRC") is still underway with its own investigation into the Government's handling of your claims. For your information, we have provided a great deal of information to the HRC about our concerns with the way in which your claims are being handled – not only by the Government, but also by the Government agencies, including the LSA, Crown Law and even the High Court.

We have seen a draft report, which we hope will be finalised within the next month or so. We had delayed issuing this newsletter in the hope that the HRC report might have been finalised by now. We are hopeful that the report, when issued, will be reasonably critical of the Government's handling of the historic abuse claims. We are also hopeful that there will be a strong recommendation made that the Government should set up a process "out of court" to deal with the claims – as has been the case in other Commonwealth countries. Once the report has been published, we will provide a synopsis of the important points on our website. For those of you who do not have access to the internet, we will eventually issue a newsletter outlining the HRC's findings and recommendations.

Listening and Assistance Service:

We have referred to the Confidential Listening and Assistance Service ("CLAS") in our last two newsletters. As we have advised you, that Service is able to hear your story and it is also able to assist you to access counselling services, both to tell your story and to deal with the abuse you have suffered. **It will not be able to provide you with an apology, or an acknowledgement as to what happened to you, or any compensation.**

In the event that you have lost the contact details for the CLAS, they are as follows: PO Box 5939, Lambton Quay, Wellington 6145, Tel. 0800 356 567, or you can look at their website at www.listening.govt.nz. We understand that the Service will be travelling throughout New Zealand and will be including visits to the prisons. If you are in prison and they will not allow you to telephone the 0800 number, please ask the prison to telephone us and we will confirm that you should be permitted to make that call.

Research: (Social Welfare cases)

In our last newsletter we referred to Dr Elizabeth Stanley's research on violence within Social Welfare homes. She continues to make progress in that regard and has interviewed a number of clients and carried out extensive research. In mid 2010, Dr Stanley travelled to Ireland to present her findings, so far, on New Zealand's handling of the historic abuse claims. Her lecture "Children, Social Welfare and State Violence in New Zealand" was well attended. The audience, which consisted mainly of Irish survivors of historic abuse, youth workers, lawyers and academics, were shocked to hear about the extent and nature of abuse suffered in New Zealand and were disappointed to learn of the Government's lack of action in that regard. A number of the Irish claimants have passed on their regards to you, as well as their encouragement that those pushing for recognition should continue with their quest to be heard and acknowledged.

We look forward to receiving the outcome of Dr Stanley's research, which is continuing through 2011. If you would like to be interviewed by Dr Stanley, she is keen to hear from more DSW claimants. The address to write to is: Elizabeth Stanley, Institute of Criminology, Victoria University of Wellington, PO Box 600, Wellington 6140.

Closing files

We remind clients that we will close files where clients have changed their contact details and we have not been updated with new contact details for 6 months or more. It is **very important** that you let us know if you change address and/or telephone number. We do not obtain that information from the LSA or the Department of Corrections. If you do not tell us your new contact details, we have no way of finding you. Where we have lost contact with a client and we have filed that client's claim in the High Court, we apply to the Court to withdraw as the lawyers on the record. The High Court requires that we advertise these applications in newspapers closest to that person's last known residence and publish the client's last known address. In cases where claims have not been filed in court and clients have not responded to our requests for contact, we send in a final invoice to the LSA and close off that client's file. Given the legal aid difficulties, it will be virtually impossible for us to re-open a client's file in that circumstance.

Mail from us

We remind you that it is important to respond to any mail that we send to you which requires some input from you. This is particularly important if your legal aid has been withdrawn. In that case, we will need you to complete forms and return them to us. That will also be the case if we are unsuccessful at LARP in overturning the Agency's decision to withdraw your legal aid and we consider you should appeal that decision.

We remind you that there will be other cases where we need you to work through draft documents that we have sent to you and which we need to complete for your case. Where we are drafting evidence for you, we will need to send completed documents to you to be formally signed and returned to us. It is important that you respond to our requests for you to help us, and that you follow the instructions we have given you.

It is also important, when we do send you documents and letters, that you understand it is sensitive and confidential information. To that end, we ask that you do not talk about the information we have provided to you, with others who were also in Social Welfare and/or psychiatric hospital care. This includes email and social networks. There is a very important reason for that. The Ministry of Health, MSD and/or Crown Law are very suspicious about the credibility of many of the claims being brought. If there is evidence that you have been discussing information we have been providing you, with others who have been in Social Welfare and/or psychiatric hospital care, then you run the risk of your credibility being damaged if that comes to light.

In addition, we note that each client's individual claim is at a different stage of progress. What is happening on one person's file will not be the same as what is happening on another, in terms of individual progress. The purpose of these newsletters, however, is to bring every client "up to speed" with the progress of work on behalf of the whole group.

Contact with this firm:

Our staff has slightly changed again. Our staff are now Sonja, Katie, Sam, Courtney, Beax and Susannah. We are always very busy progressing work. As per usual, Beax will typically be your first port of call. We remind you that she has a good working knowledge of every client's file and is a qualified legal executive. Where Beax is unable to assist you, she will be able to refer you to one of the solicitors.

As we have stated in other newsletters, we do try to keep your costs down as much as possible. That will mean that we may not reply to every letter you send in to us. It may also mean that we do not return some toll calls, particularly where you are simply looking for an update. We will let you know, via letter or telephone call, of any important news that affects your claim.

We do know that many of you are frustrated about what seems to be a lack of progress with your claims. So are we. We are working hard to try and change that and we are making some progress, as we have set out in this newsletter. We ask that you bear with us. If you are finding it all too hard, however, just let us know and we will take steps to

close off your file with us. We suggest, in that case, that you keep an eye on our website for news about out of court developments that may arise as a result of the HRC report. We will be sure to add to the site the outcome of the HRC report, as well as any information which is of interest to the client group. That site can be found at [illegible].co.nz.

We also encourage you to complain to your local MPs, the Ministry of Justice (Simon Power), and also the Human Rights Commission about the Government's lack of progress in dealing with historic abuse claims.

Summary:

To summarise, it has been a reasonably difficult 7-8 months. The LSA has escalated the withdrawal of our clients' legal aid, as is evident from the newsletter. We have also had unexpected decisions from LARP which have been unfavourable to our clients and which we are now having to appeal. On the bright side, however, we have the first sign that there may be some movement towards settlement of some clients' claims. In that regard, we refer to the agreement to trial the claims through the JSC process in the High Court. We can only hope that we will start settling more of your claims and we will keep you advised as to progress.

We are also pleased that the HRC should soon issue its report into the Government's handling of your claims. We are hopeful that the report, which will not only go to the United Nations, but also to the Government, will finally result in a proper process being set up to provide you with compensation and services for the abuse you have suffered in care.

We want to let you know that although we are a small team, we are very determined to achieve an outcome that recognises the abuse you have suffered and ensures that you receive an acknowledgement and compensation for that. We work hard to achieve that outcome and we do feel that we are now making some progress with that. Thank you for your continued support for our work, which we hope will produce positive outcomes for you in the not too distant future.

Regards, Sonja & Team

Important note:
This newsletter is intended solely for the information of claimants. It is not, and is not intended as a substitute for, legal advice. We strongly recommend that you keep the contents of this newsletter confidential.

COOPER LEGAL INFORATION LETTER

COOPER LEGAL
Barristers and Solicitors

Level 1
Gleneagles Building
69-71 The Terrace
Wellington
PO Box 10609
The Terrace, Wellington 6143
Telephone: 04-499 9025
Fax: 04-499 9299
Email: sonja@cooperlegal.co.nz

S M Cooper
October 2010

Dear Client

As you will be aware, we have been spending a large amount of time dealing with problems with the Legal Services Agency, over the past two and half years. The work involved in dealing with the Legal Services Agency's withdrawal of aid process, combined with this work we have been required to do on individual claims to comply with timetables has meant that we have been unable to carry out much correspondence with clients. Please be reassured that we are working hard to protect your legal rights and attempt to get legal aid continued for you. For more information in relation to the legal aid situation and progress of the claims generally, please see the **enclosed** newsletter.

Please find **enclosed** copies of invoices and/or amendment to grant documents which have been sent to the Legal Services Agency over the course of this year.

Where we have sent an invoice, it means that we have carried out work on your file which has been necessary as part of the litigation process or else to comply with work that we have had to do to fight the Legal Services Agency's withdrawal of aid process for each client.

Where an amendment to grant has been sent to the Agency, that document has been forwarded as a request for funding beyond what is already available on the file. For example, we have been submitting funding requests for the next steps required to be undertaken on individual files, such as drafting documents or collecting in records on your behalf. In other cases, the invoice has been above the available funding (because of extra time needed to complete the relevant work) and we have had to forward an amendment to grant to cover the overrun.

Where the Legal Services Agency has paid or declined to pay an invoice, or considered and approved and/or declined an amendment to grant application for further funding, it will have notified you of that by letter. This process can take quite some considerable time, however, so any letter may relate to an invoice or amendment to grant sent some months earlier. Alternatively, the Legal Services Agency may have yet to consider the documents and you will receive a letter in relation to that at some stage in the future. If some of the documents seem to be duplicated, it is because the Legal Services Agency has, in some instances, required us to re-submit amendments to grant.

The documents are for your information only and you are not required to take any action at this stage. We understand that letters and documents relating to the Legal Services Agency can be incomprehensible, at times. Please telephone the Agency directly if you have questions relating to your legal aid situation.

Yours sincerely

Sonja M Cooper
Principal

Legal Services Agency

Civil/Family Legal Aid
Amendment to Grant

3/07 form 9

Legal aid file no.
Lead provider's reference

Name of aided person: DARRYL SMITH
Name of lead provider: SORUI.M COOPER
Name of law firm: COOPER LEGAL
Fixture category: [ ] 1 [ ] 2 [ ] 3 [X] 4

Type of proceedings this amendment covers: CIVIL HIGH COURT
This amendment is for step(s): AMEND PLEADINGS (AP)   enter invoice direct

		Lead Provider		Listed Provider B		Listed Provider C	
Provider name or number		5795		17865			
Level of experience							
Enter the step that best fits with work to be completed		Hours	Total Fee	Hours	Total Fee	Hours	Total Fee
Step	AP	Preparation time	$ 1,736.00	$		$	
Step		Hearing time	$	$		$	
Step		Preparation time	$	$		$	
Step		Hearing time	$	$		$	
Step		Preparation time	$	$		$	
Step		Hearing time	$	$		$	
Other (specify)			$	$		$	
			$	$		$	
Totals		8.00	$1,736.00	0.00	$	0.00	$ 0.00

Total Fees (incl. GST) $ 1,736.00

Disbursements (specify)	ONGOING OFFICE COSTS	$100.00
		$
		$
		$

Total disbursements (incl. GST) $ 100.00
Total amount sought (incl. GST) $ 1,836.00

[ ] Approve [ ] Further information [ ] Refuse

Name

Comments

Signature

Date
    day   month   year

page 1

PHOTOS OF ME MEETING THE CHIEF EXECUTIVE OFFICER OF MINISTRY OF SOCIAL DEVELOPMENT RECEIVING LETTER IN 2012

CAMPBELL PARK SCHOOL MAGAZINES 1976 TO 1977

Campbell Park School

MAGAZINE

1976

STAFF

Principal:	P G Aspden
Assistant Principal	P F Walsh
Senior Housemasters:	B E Mansfield
	B L Walsh
Housemasters:	Henderson, P
	Goodwin, P
	Wardell, D H
	Parsons, P
	Mathers, T J
Assistant Housemasters:	Forrester, J
	Taylor, B V
	Worling, R
	Albers, C
	Lee, R M
	Chave, R
Matron:	Mrs I F Willis
Sub-Matron:	Mrs M C Andrews
Cottage Matrons:	Mrs N I Irvine
	Miss N Savage
	Mrs E Jackways
Cottage sub-Matrons:	Mrs D W Adams
	Mrs G G Campbell
	Mrs E Worling
Matrons Assistants:	Mrs C Middlemass
	Mrs G M Hughes
	Miss D Foster
	Mrs R McCullough
	Mrs J McKenzie
	Mrs W Carter
Senior Clerk:	Mrs D Bright
Clerks:	R B Malthus
	Mrs N A Frannie
Clerical Assistant:	Mrs J D Hogan
Typist:	Ms A D Gray

Senior Teacher:	S B Willis
Teachers:	Miss J E Gibson
	B L Waddell
	J E Turner
	N F O'Connor
	Miss K McCone
	Mrs E Rylance
	Mrs D Johnson
Manual Training:	G Gilchrist
Teachers' Aide:	Mrs A Mansfield
Head Cook:	S C Mans
Cooks:	Mrs J Baird
	S F Adams
Seamstress:	Mrs B M Curtis
Laundresses:	Mrs E M Sullivan
	Mrs E B Linwood
Engineer:	L Clyne
Boilermen:	L I McCullough
	G F Russell
	B I Thompson
Instructors:	
Carpenters:	A J H Curtis
	D M E Harris
Painter:	C R Sutton
Bootmaker:	A B Earls
Gardener:	L V Linwood
Poultry:	J A R Johnssen
Grounds:	S Juckes
Driver:	Miss D M McAuley
Night Attendants	W S Russell
	L Irvine
	A Jackways
	B Wollen

3.

CAMPBELL PARK AND THE COMMUNITY

Visits, functions, outings and contacts with outside organisations

February

13   Taylor House colour television installed after almost three years of effort.

14   Dansey House hike to Mt Jackson.

17   Visit from Island and Maori Affairs Department Officers.

18   Psychologists visiting for assessment.

22   Weekend camp at Timaru for six Dansey House boys.

23   Visit by Windsor C.W.I.

23-27   Vocational Class on extended trip to Lake Ohau.

23   Upper Waitaki Schools swimming sports.

28   Evening visit by Rev. Bruce and Oamaru Baptist group - items and discussion.

29   Visit by Innerwheel, Rotaract and Rotary Clubs - games, afternoon tea and presentation of books.

March

1-5   Room 5 extended trip to Lake Ohau.

4   Party of boys fishing with Mr Bruce Holt.

6   24 boys to concert at Otekaike.

9   Four boys competed in the North Otago swimming Championships.

27   Visit by Salvation Army group. Afternoon - cricket, concert at night.

28   Presbyterian boys to Kurow Church Service followed by lunch and afternoon with Kurow families.

31   Upper Waitaki district schools softball tournament held at Campbell Park.

April

3   Visit by ten trainee psychologists from Auckland.

4   Visit by Mr Peak and Timaru Hospital Laundry staff. Cricket v Campbell House.

5-8   Room 1 boys on extended trip to Timaru.

11   Dansey House boys to Oamaru as guests of the Rotary Club.

13   Visit by Round Table group.

14   Kurow Area School combined with Senior Section and Room 5 boys for athletics at Campbell Park.

14-20   Taylor House camp at Aviemore.

18   Campbell House to rugby match at Kurow.

23   Visit by Youth Aid Officer, Timaru, Constable Hendry.

June

1	Visit to Campbell House by Round Table group.
8	Visit to Taylor House by Enfield C.W.I.
8-10	Psychologists visiting for assessment.
9	Indoor Bowls v St Lukes at Oamaru.
15	Mr O'Connor and class attended Gymnastics course, at Campbell Park.
21-23	Visit by special class teachers from Christchurch.
23	Upper Waitaki Schools soccer tournament at Kurow.
27	Taylor House afternoon bus trip.

July

2	Church of England boys to St Mary's A.A.W. Oamaru. Tea and indoor games.
4	Church of England boys to St Luke's A.A.W. Oamaru. Church service, lunch, outing with families.
7	Visit by Rotaract club to Dansey House.
11	Dansey House afternoon bus trip.
12	Visit by two Central Otago Principals and two Social Welfare Officers.
14	Indoor bowls at Oamaru v W.H.P.B. Trophy won by Campbell Park.
18	Taylor House all day trip to Hakm Valley.
19	First Aid course run by St John's, Kurow, on weekly basis for ten Dansey House boys.
25	Rugby v Twizel at Campbell Park. Won by Twizel. 41 - 32.
26	Visit by Ardgowan W.D.P.P. to Taylor and Dansey houses.
30	Thirty boys to Oamaru to the Gang Show.

August

1	Visit by Oamaru and Twizel Maori Groups. Rugby. Concert in hall.
8	Rotary Interhouse relay race.
11	Music Festival, Oamaru.
13	10 - aside rugby tournament, Kurow.
17	Twizel School pupils visited. Rugby and basketball.
18	Kurow Area School playing rugby.

September

13	Dansey House colour television installed.
16	Visit from Rev. B Kingi
19	Jim Craik memorial barbecue unveiled by Rotary Club, Oamaru.
20	Twenty boys to Oamaru as guests of Rotary Club.
22	Upper Waitaki Schools cross country at Otematata. Psychologists visiting for assessment.
26	Six Church of England boys to Confirmation Service at Kurow.

October

4	Members of Rothmans Under 21 team visit for lunch and a coaching session.
10	Presbyterian boys to Kurow Church Service, lunch and outing.
13	Mini Athletics at Kurow.
15	Visit by Oamaru W.D.F.F. to Dansey House.
17	Taylor House all day trip to Dansey's Pass.
20	Visit from Hydatids Control Officer.
25	Morning performance by the "Potter's People" religious pop group.
30	Otago Schools championship athletic sports.
31	Presbyterian and O.B. boys to Duntroon Church Service and lunch.
	Visit by Rev. B Wilkinson and Anglican families.

November

4	Visit by Windsor C.W.I.
	Twenty Campbell House boys to Timaru as guests of Timaru Hospital laundry staff.
	Forty boys attended the Twizel Rep. Societies presentation of "H.M.S. Pinafore" at Kurow.
6	Anti-litter drive to Duntroon.
7	Visit by Oamaru Maori Committee: Rangi, softball, cricket, concert.
9	Visit by Glenavy C.W.I.
14	Visit by Twizel Maori Women's Welfare League.
16	Upper Waitaki Inter-School athletic Sports at Campbell Park.
20	Visit by Kurow Cubs. Tabloid sports v Taylor House.
21	Dansey House hike up Mt. Otekaike.
23	Visit by St Stephen's College boys. Items.
27	Annual Cross-country run.
28	Roman Catholic boys to Oamaru. Church Service, lunch and outing with families.
	Twenty boys to Oamaru as guests of Rotary Club.

December

2	Religious instruction break-up.
6	Winning house and of year function.
8	Annual steeplechase.
10	Combined Dansey-Taylor House end of term function.
11	Visit by Tas E.

SOCCER

On July 29 two soccer teams went to Kurow, to a
soccer tournament. We took an A team and a B team.
The A team won both games and the B team lost both of
their games. The A team played Kurow and they won
1 - nil. Then they played Duntroon and they won
2 - nil. I scored two goals. The second game which
we played was the finals and we won it. There were six
schools there. Everybody enjoyed the games. On the
way back Mr O'Connor and the boys went to his house and
we got an apple each. Then we came back to Campbell Park.

Raymond CASEY   13 years

GYMNASTICS

At Campbell Park, Mr & Mrs Crosbie take boys for
gymnastics on Tuesday nights from half past six until
half past seven. Mr Byrtles from Oamaru used to come
out and help us, but he doesn't now. He only comes when
we are ready for badges. You have to get an iron badge
before you can get bronze and after bronze you can get a
silver. Silver is the highest you can get. About twelve
boys got badges last term. Patrick KORA and Eric SMITH
are the best gymnasts   so far this term. We have bar
work and mat work and box work. It is good fun. We have
powder for bar work. Mr Crosbie sends away for the powder.
It is made in Auckland.

Raymond CASEY   13 years

INTER SCHOOL CHAMPIONSHIPS

Three of us went to Dunedin for the sports on Saturday
morning. I got up, put on my clothes and went to breakfast
with Patrick and Peter. Then Mr Turner came and we had
breakfast. After breakfast Mr T rner gave me the keys to
get the cups in the classroom. Then I went down to his
place and he was just hanging his washing out before we
went. Then Mr Johansen brought his son and we left to go
to Dunedin and on our way there Mr Turner told us where
Mr Waddell had his house and showed us where Mrs Rylance
lived. Then we went past Mr Gilchrist's house. On our
way there we saw Mr Mearns giving the mail out and he told
us he was going to play cricket. Then we went to sports
and Patrick KORA and I were in the first event, the high
jump. we missed the bars on the second jump but did very
well. After that we went to a park and we had lunch there.

SOFTBALL TOURNAMENT AT CAMPBELL PARK

This year lots of schools came to Campbell Park
School to play soft-ball. It was played in the first
term. We had the Room 8 boys umpiring all the games.
After the first two rounds we had lunch under the big
walnut tree. All of the teachers came to the tournament
to watch their schools play against Campbell Park boys.
Our top team beat the Otamatata team to win the competition.
They had some good Maori girls playing for them.

James RANGIRANGI 14 years

****

WAR

I was at home in U.S.A. Next minute my door bell
rang, and there was a man from the Air Force. He asked
me if I would like to join the Air Force. I said "Yes".
I was trained to be a pilot and I was there for six years
training. I flew a bomber for U.S.A. I was told that
there was a war coming up soon.

The day came when I had to go to the war to fight
for my country. War broke out. Every body went mad.
I was posted to England then we had to make night-raids
on Germany. One night was very rough, we just managed
to drop a load of bombs. My plane just about was out of
bombs when some bullets hit one my engines. It went on
fire. The crew and I parachuted to the ground. Some
German officers found me and my crew in a stolen truck.
We managed to kill some German Officers and then some
men surrounded me and my crew. They were German Officers.
We had no chance of getting away so we gave up. We were
taken to a prison called Colditz; the prison was like a
castle; we was there until the war was over. I escaped
from Colditz with flight Lieutenant P Curran. We got to
Sweden and then we went to U.S.A. and asked my boss what
it was like over there. I told him the plane. My boss
asked me if I would like to go back there with him and I
said "Yes, I would like to."

Ricky BURTON 10 years

PETS IN THE HALL

On the 24th September, we all took our pets down to the hall to get judged. Mr Aspden and Mr Walsh and all kinds of other people were there. There were cows pigs, chickens, cats, dogs, sheep, horses, and some other things. All of the school went down to see the pets. After they were judged Mr Walsh and the people walked around for a long time till they got to the one they though was the best. The winner was Darren MUIR. The winner got a bottle of large. I liked the show and the pets very much. I thought they were very nice.

David McLINTOCK   14 years

MY PET

My pet's name is Fido. He is all brown. He is one year and nine months old. He likes people who are good to him. He was born in New Zealand. He can fight and he has blue eyes. He has got one blind eye. He got the blind eye by getting a stone in it. His birthday is on September 24th. He likes playing in the water. Every body in Dunedin comes along and pays 5 cents to see him, because he is a lovely dog. Every body says to each other "I wouldn't mind having that dog for a pet. He goes hunting with me. When I have shot a pig or a rabbit or a duck, he goes and gets them and brings them back to me. Everywhere I go around the farm Fido comes too. He rounds up all the sheep for me. He gets fed three times a day. He gets meat and milk. He doesn't do anything wrong. He has four legs and one tail. He has four teeth down the bottom and four teeth up the top. Every morning and afternoon he goes down to the gate and gets the papers. He likes playing with other dogs. Every time I go for a walk I take Fido because I know that he wants to come. So I let him come. He goes with me down to the shop. Fido can eat a wee bit of ice-cream some times.

Raymond CASEY   13 years

HUNTING

To go hunting first you have to have the right sort
of clothes and food and some extras for emergencies.
Before you go you will have to make sure you pick a good
clear day. Next you must be sure you know how to use
your weapon extremely well and check that it is in good
order before using it. Anyway two men and a lady went
hunting and had all that they wanted and enough food to
last the day. But there was something else these three
people had forgotten - to bring a compass along with them.
John, Mark and Mary were in the bush and enjoying the nice
warm day. John stopped and got his rifle ready but he
forgot to check that every thing was well and the gun was
in good order. He was too careless and didn't care.

Gradually, they got deeper into the woods where every
thing was quiet and all they heard was the chirp of the
birds and the rustle of the leaves. They stopped and rested
for a while and had something to eat and soon they were on
their way again and were getting further and further into
the woods. They had just got to a little stream to drink
when they heard a sound across from them. Mark looked up
and saw a wild boar snorting and digging the ground with
his nose, but he hadn't noticed the people. John pulled
out his rifle and aimed at the pig, but at that moment
the pig looked at them and slowly walked up to the people.
Mark called out to John to shoot but before he could he
was hit by the pig and then he went flying into the ferns.
Mark and Mary ran and found a tree to climb. They got up
the tree and looked back down at the pig, and then back
at John.

The pig slowly walked away and Mary called out to
John but there was no answer from him. They got off the
tree and went over to him, they rolled him over and saw
that he had been hit in the head and was killed. Mary
started crying and Mark tried to keep her warm and happy
but it didn't help her. They both started out of the bush
but it was getting darker and darker. They stopped in the
bush for a rest. Mark said to Mary that they might as well
sleep in the bush so that is how it ended because they were
lost and they had also lost their mate; because of care-
lessness.

Peter MEREWINI   14 years

MY DOG

I take Snoopy for walks down the beach, sometime he goes for a swim and he does not like it when I tell him to come out. When Dad comes home he barks at him and he always runs down the road and goes after cats, but when my brother tells him to go to bed he comes inside and sleeps under our bed. When Shane gets up he goes outside and calls Snoopy. If he is not there Shane sings out to him and he comes out the door. Sometimes Shane and I take Snoopy down to the park and Snoopy runs after us all the time but he knows that he shouldn't do that. When my friend comes around he comes up to the television and watches it until it is bed time. There are ten boys that Snoopy likes and plays with but he does not like girls. Now I can't see him at all because he has died, but Dad might buy another dog for us again.

Mark HADDON 14 years

THE PET I FOUND

Once upon a time I found a dog and it was very sad. It was cold and shaking so I took it home with me. He was warming up by the fire while I was getting him something to eat and drink. He was brown and small, fat and long. I looked at his collar and it had no address on it and then I didn't know what to do so I rang the S.P.C.A. and it was engaged, so I waited. I rang up again and somebody answered the phone and they told me that there was a reward for it so I took it down to the S.P.C.A. and the owners were waiting for me to bring the dog. They gave me the reward and then they said "Thank you for looking after it" and they were very grateful and proud of me. They gave me a very good reward.

Arthur KELLY 13 years

RESCUED BY MY PET

Once upon a time on a fine summer day I decided to take a walk with my pet dog named King. He has a very big German Shepherd and he always liked to go for walks after he had something to eat. Soon King and I were on our way through the bush and across swamps and rivers. We were going along a cliffy side on a mountain slope with a very steep drop. As we walked along the top of this cliff, King noticed a figure in the far distance. King started to bark and pant and soon he started to get very vicious. I tried to see what he was barking at but it was too far for me to see. When I looked around King was gone and I was all alone. Not far from where I stopped I was face to face with a wild pig. I tried to walk back slowly but I tripped and soon the wild pig was on top of me. I felt one of its fangs going into my legs. The pain was terrible and it was no use there was nothing much I could do.

As I was on the ground I heard a bark. I looked
around and I saw King and three other dogs. I said to myself, King must have known there was going to be trouble
so he went to get some help. The four dogs were fighting
the wild pig and when the fight was over King came up to
me and I hung on to him and went home safely. From then on
King went with me everywhere I went.

Peter MEREWINI   14 years

MY PET

One day when I went to the Park to have a swim a
yellow duck came swimming by and I picked it up and it
sounded as if it was lost. So I let it go. Then I went
home. On my way home the little duck followed me so I
put it by the fire and it started to say "quack-quack".
Then I gave it some food and it went to sleep.

The next day the duck was half dead. The cat had
got in to it so I took it to the vet. For a couple of
days I kept it in the cage and gave it a feed every day
and it got better and better. When I and my foster parents
went on a trip I took the duck with me. The duck swam in
the water and it was so happy it swam out in to the lake.
When I swam out after it, it swam away and died in the
water where it belongs and some other duck came along so
we left it and went home and I never got another duck again.

Thomas SAVAGE   13 years

SAVED BY MY PET

One day I went for a walk to the bush with my pet dog
to look for some mushrooms, then I went home for my lunch.
The next morning I asked my mother if I could go camping.
My mother said "Yes" and then she packed my lunch and I
made my way to the camp. When I arrived in the camping
grounds the man said that dogs were not allowed in the
camping grounds.   I begged and begged him to let my dog
stay and then he said "Yes" and I was happy.

The next morning my dog and I went for a walk in the
bush. I took my lunch with me. As it grew darker it began
to get colder and colder until I lit a fire, so I could
keep warm. I fell asleep and the fire was still burning
and suddenly a big wind came across and blew a lot of leaves
in to the fire. Then another big wind came across and blew
some burning leaves across the bush and then it caught fire
on the other leaves on the ground. My dog smelt the smoke
from the fire. My dog barked and barked and he licked me
and he tried to wake me up. I finally woke up and I started

to cough, and then I smelt the smoke. I saw the fire
across the bush. I ran as fast as I could back to the
camp and saw the owner and told him about the fire. The
owner called all the people in the camping ground to get
as many sacks as they could. We all ran as fast as we
could to the fire, but when we got there the fire was put
out, but it was still smoking when the smoke cleared. I
saw my dog sitting there with a wet bag near his side. My
dog had put the fire out all by himself, he had saved my
life and the people's lives too. It never moved and I knew
it had died.

Moana CASH 14 years

BILLIARDS:

. Billiards is an indoor game for all ages. It is
played with three small heavy balls, two white ones with
a black spot and a red. The first player strikes his own
ball with or without a spot then with a long stick called
a cue. He gets points if he bounces his ball off another
into a pocket. If he knocks a ball into a pocket with his
own in one shot he gets points for a cannon.

    I haven't played billiards for a long time but I like
to have a good game when I can. Before I came here I used
to go into the billiards saloon to play with my mates. They
used to think that I was eighteen.

Fred WAIKAI 15 years

HUNTED BY GREEDY MEN:

    The greedy men hunted for a White Stallion which had
run away from the other horses which were mares and they
hunted and hunted for it. The first time they caught the
horse by rope in the Corral. They caught it all right but
the rope around his neck broke and the horse galloped away.
Later the boy found it. So he took it home.   When he
caught it and he hopped on it and away he went. He cared
for it and fed it.

    One day while the White Stallion was tied up three
men came looking for it. They had the mares with them and
they were rounding them up. They were not very far away
from the boy's house. His sister was feeding the stallion
and the boy was taking care of his because of his foot; it
was bleeding so he fixed it up. The mares came past and they
made a noise as they came by and the stallion heard the calls
of the mares. The boy told his sister to move from the horse
and she did. The boy tried to hop on so the stallion but he
couldn't and the horse heard the mares call. So he reared up
and broke the rope and it smashed the fence and then went
away with the other mares.

14.

The boy was very worried as he went to look for it.
He went out in his boat and he looked in the swamp and he
found it. The men were also looking for it, but they
couldn't find it so they smoked him out. The boy saw the
smoke and then he saw the horse and so he hopped on. It
took off out of the smoke and the chase began. The men
hopped on their horses and chased him but they couldn't
find him so they kept on hunting for the boy and the horse.

The boy saw a rabbit and he went to chase it. He
caught it and lit a fire and cooked it but just as he went
to eat it, who should arrive but the greedy men who wanted
the horse. The boy saw them and he hopped on the horse
and the chase started again. They ran a long way and they
went on and on to the sea.

Arthur. KELLY   13 years

PEDRO AND THE WHITE STALLION

My story is based on Pedro who showed so much love
and care for the White Stallion. The White Stallion was
a very proud horse and was very wild. The White Stallion
was leading a herd of mares and he continued being leader.
This stallion was a very good looking horse, with a long
straight flowing mane. The three men who were looking
after the horse liked this stallion very much but the horse
didn't seem to like them. The White Stallion gave these
men a very tough time because they kept trying to catch him.
The three men were very mad that they couldn't catch the
White Stallion so they tried to trap him by leading him
into a big round corral. The stallion went into the corral
and was trapped. The three men got a rope and tried to
put it around the White Stallion's neck. The men had
finally got the rope on but that did not stop the horse from
jumping around. The White Stallion was so wild that the
three men were just not enough to try and stop the stallion
from jumping.

Pedro who was a small fisherman was watching the way
these three men treated the White Stallion. Pedro did not
like the way these three men were treating the horse, but
he just watched the cruel men lash at him. The stallion
broke away from the three men and climbed through the two
poles that the men used to keep the stallion in.

The White Stallion was free and was running wild again,
but this time he did not go back to the herd of mares. He
just went his own way and was free. The three men rode off
on their horses after the White Stallion and Pedro watched
them going out in to the far swamp. Pedro turned back and
went home to get something to eat.

He got back to his father's house which was isolated from a lot of people and many friends, but Pedro didn't seem to worry because he had a father and a little sister. Pedro loved his little sister but he had more on his mind. After having something to eat Pedro went off to sleep and he had a small dream about the White Stallion. He dreamt that the White Stallion was his friend and was not wild. He dreamt that wherever he went the White Stallion would follow him up the beach. Pedro woke up looking a bit sad.

Pedro's father was asleep so he slowly sneaked off and got a rope to try and catch the White Stallion. Pedro was now out to catch the stallion and he was determined to catch it. As he was looking around the swamp for the White Stallion he stopped at a bridge to look at a net that he and his father had set to catch fish to eat. There were quite a few fish in the net. Pedro carried on down the swamp trying to find the horse. As he went he saw the stallion in the swamp behind a tree. Pedro slowly sneaked up on the horse and tried to throw his rope over the White Stallion. The stallion took off and left Pedro standing there. Pedro heard horse feet stamping behind him, he looked around and saw the three men who wanted the stallion. Pedro soon knew why the stallion had run off. Pedro put his head down and he tried his best not to weep. Later Pedro and the stallion became friends but they were both hunted by the three men and eventually the film ended with their death. It was a sad but true film and I wish in a way that I'd been Pedro.

Peter MENERINI   14 years

****

SNOW

Snow drops down from the sky.
Snow covers all the houses and road.
Snow is very soft to walk in.
Snow sometimes gets a crust and is crunchy.
Snow is very white and it even covers the grass.
Snow is beautiful.
Snow can be fun.
Snow is comfortable.
Snow shows your tracks behind you.
Snow is good fun to play in.
Snow can be thrown at other people.
Snow is nice around the place.

Michael WILSON   14 years

SNOW

Snow can be very slippery after heavy rain. Today it is very cold here. The roads around the country are very dangerous. Campbell Park School is covered with snow today. The sun is shining now. In Christchurch the roads around Christchurch are very slippery. Slippery conditions can cause accidents on the road.

Snow can feel cold after eating it. Snow can get worse after a bad storm. Snow can also block roads around the hills like Porters Pass, and Arthurs Pass, Otira, the Lewis Pass, and high-way between the Waipara turn off to Hanmer Springs turn off. Around Kaikoura it is very slippery around the Banderlees.

Traffic can cause a big problem on the roads, people can go skiing on the slopes. The roads can get worse after snow which has been falling for two days. Paddocks can get very slippery and muddy after heavy snow and rain. People can throw snowballs at each other. Cars can skid and roll over in icy patches on the road. It can get colder and get worse during the day and night. People have to drive at about 20 miles per hour on the roads.

Gary McLENNAGHEN   15 years

SNOW

It is snowing here today and the snow is piling up by our cottage. I like snow because it is beautiful and sometimes you can eat it. Snow is cold, yesterday when we got back from our trip we made snow balls and threw them at each other. Some people threw them at the bus. We were hoping that we could sledge down the hill. When the sun comes up the snow will melt into water. When you play in the snow you could cause a lot of damage because there might be stones in it. Snow never makes a noise but it is sad when the snow goes.

Ricky JONATHAN   14 years

****

GANG

A gang is men who go around on bikes, some of them have got jobs and go in the gang on their days off. Girls can be in a gang with boys. There are good gangs and bad gangs too. The bad gangs go around scaring people and the men in the gang haven't had a bath for about nine weeks too. I think gangs are dumb. I would not go and be in a gang. I would not join this group of people because they get into too much trouble with the law.

Mark HIGGINS   14 years

GANGS

I once joined a gang with my big brother. The first
thing I had to do was to sign this paper. My brother was
a leader of the big Hells Angels. They were one man short.
Mach Friday I went to the dances and picked up this girl.
She was pretty. One night as I played in the band I heard
her screaming so I walked off the stage and said "step outside mate". The man was 16 so he did. He kicked me in
the guts and I fell down. Junior came out and said "get
stuck in", so I did. I punched his face and kicked his
head. He picked up a bottle and as he was going to break
it open my brother stopped his hand and picked him up by
the neck and put him in the gutter. The boy gave up and
went home and that was my day's work. I was tired so I
went to sleep.

                    Ricky JONATHAN 14 years

                    ****

WORK AT CAMPBELL PARK SCHOOL

While we are in bed the housemaster comes to waken
us up. After we have made our beds we go up and have a
wash. After we have had our wash we go up top and wait
for the whistle and when the whistle has gone we go down
and line up and we have our breakfast. After breakfast
we line up for assembly and we go in and sit down. Mr
Aspden tells us how we have been.

After Taylor and Ramsay houses have gone out Mr Walsh
calls out the names of the work places. When I am called
out for the farm Matiu TAI and I go down to the farmer's
shed and we check the petrol and water. Then we bring out
the tractor. This is on a Thursday, and we take the tractor
and put the trailer on it and we go up top and get the
rubbish from the cottages and we get the rubbish from the
school; we go down and stop to pick up the bin from the
Administration Block. Me and Matiu take it over to the
incinerator and Mr Robertson brings over the tractor and
we clean out the incinerator, tip out the rubbish and we
go and take the bins back to the cottages and we go back
down. We go and get some soil and we fill the hole with
the soil until the whistle goes. We go up to smoke.
After Smoko we go down and get some more soil. After that
we have to go and fill up the hole and we level out the
hole with soil. Time was running short to go up for lunch.

When we had finished our lunch we went back to work.
We had a look at the soil and we check on the mower and
went down to see which lawn needed mowing and we mowed
paddock 7 and when I had finished it then I mowed paddock
8. Time was running fast and I stopped for smoko.

We went down to collect the rubbish around the house.
After we had been to the last house we stuck on the tar-
paulin and we went down to the dump. When we got to the
dump we dumped our rubbish and we burnt our rubbish and
then we made our way back. When we got back we washed down
the truck and Mr Robertson put the truck away and the
whistle went. We went up for tea and I went and washed
my hands ready for tea.

After we went and polished our boots and   had our
showers. We had to wait for the housemaster to come to
check our drawers and we went up top and some boys played
pool and billiards and some boys went to watch television.
When it was time for the meeting we all went up .top and
when Mr Mansfield came up for the meeting he said "Evening
boys", he told us about our reports. When the meeting was
finished some boys watched television and some boys went
to bed.

Walter RUKA   13 years.

OUR TRIP TO TIMARU

We left Campbell Park and went to Timaru and we went
to the Woollen Mills on the same day. Then we went to the
camping ground and unpacked our gear into our huts. Then
we went to have a look around the shops, and then we came
back up to the camping ground and cooked tea. After that
we watched television. Then we had some supper, watched
some more television and then we came back and did our
diaries and then went to bed.

We went to the radio staion on Tuesday morning and
it was fun. A man showed us how it worked. There were
a lot of recbords in the station. We went to the telephone
exchange on Tuesday at 10.00. We saw hundreds of wires
and we saw some telephones.

Then we went to the game park at 11.30 a.m. where
we had our lunch. We saw ponies, chickens, ducks, donkeys,
bisons, goats, monkeys, peacocks, and other animals.
There were two cougas there. After the game park we went
to the freezing works. The first place we went to was
where they keep them over-night. Then we saw a truck coming in to unload the sheep. We went to the killing part
and saw men cutting their throats and breaking their necks.
We moved along a bit and we saw them pulling their skins
off; we moved further along and we saw them cutting the
sheep open and we could see all the stomach. We then moved
to another room and it was where they cut them into
quarters and stamp them. We saw some men wrapping the
meat up. Then we went back to the freezer and we saw
lots of sheep.

We went back to the camping ground and had some tea,
and watched Six Million Dollar Man. Then we had supper
and went to bed.

ROOM 8 VISITS TIMARU

On Monday our class went to Timaru with Mr J Waddell. We went in the mini-bus. We left after assembly and arrived there about 11.30 a.m. The first place we went to was Hame Industries and we played table-tennis, darts and draughts and Mr McFarlane gave us a drink and some chips. We went into the main building and then saw the steel rollers.

When we went to the Hospital Laundry, Mr Peak showed us around. The first place we went to was the laundry. It was very hot inside, two ladies were washing lots of clothes. After that we went to the place where they keep baby clothes. It was hot inside there too. Mr Peak showed us the sewing room last and they were making clothes.

We had lunch at the harbour. For lunch we had egg sandwiches, ham sandwiches and a drink; after that we had some biscuits and an orange. We went for a walk by the ship and saw a lot of small fish. After that Mr Waddell went back to get the mini-bus and then we went to Parks and Reserves.

We arrived at Parks and Reserves about two o'clock and Mr Scott showed us the glass house first and there were pretty flowers too. After that we went into the room and all the boys washed their hands. Afterwards we went to the glass house. Mr Scott was bedding out into the gardens. There was also a water sprinkler and then we went back to the mini-bus. Mr Scott gave us some plants.

When we arrived at the family home the lady gave us a drink and two biscuits. After that we played in the garden. Me and Peter McKenzie washed the dishes and had a short game of pool.

When it was time to go back we went to the Oamaru Family Home. Miss Timaru bought an ice-cream and we arrived at Campbell Park about six o'clock.

Ricky JONATHAN   14 years

HAME INDUSTRIES

We went to Timaru for the day and we went to Hame to have a look around where the boys work.

We went to have a look at their safety precautions. They wear goggles and helmets and steel tipped boots and ear plugs to keep the noise out and have safety posters on the walls for the men to read. We went to have a look at the other men and what they were doing. One man was joining two bits of steel together. In the other room one man who was showing us around the places said "Do you want to see how we make them round?" and the boys said "Yes". First he was showing us these buttons and there was this big handle sticking out and he said "This handle is for making it go forwards and back and this one is a button

Wednesday we got up and had a wash and went down to the kitchen and cooked breakfast. Then we had grace and the boys who were late for breakfast had to do the dishes. We got in the mini and went to the car museum. Eric SMITH had two dollars worth of fish and chips.

Raymond CASEY   13 years

EASTER AT FISHERMAN'S BEND

On Easter Weekend Taylor House went for a camping trip to Aviemore Dam and we slept on lilos and in sleeping bags and tents. There were four tents. We had house competitions each morning and we had tent inspections and after that we had free time and we had morning tea and after that we had free time again.

On Saturday Mrs Crosbie came to see how camp was going and she brought Mr Crosbie's kites and I flew one and Shane flew one too. The others played cricket and soccer.

Beverly played with Jason and Dominic and James and Rex. On Sunday we took the canoe down to the river and we had a ride in it but me and Jason stayed with some visitors all afternoon. Well we came back on Tuesday and got everything off, the trailer clean, and we had showers and went off to tea.

Thomas SAVAGE   13 years

THE LAUNDRY

At the laundry Mr Peek showed us around. First we went up to the top to see the women sorting out the clothes and then down where they wash and iron them. Mr Peek showed us a spin-dryer and then he showed us where they put the clothes and then we went to the sewing room where the women make some clothes. One of the women cut the shape and then sewed the material.

Robert BURNS   15 years

WHAKATANE

I live in Whakatane. It is a fairly small town.
There is a bank, hotels, playground, picture theatres,
and a very good rowing club. Some of the Olympic rowers
come from Whakatane. I watch them practicing. I live
near the harbour and there are a lot of yachts and rowing
boats. There are plenty of fishermen. They walk through
Wairakapa, where they speak Maori. I have been to a Maori
funeral there.

Michael NEWTON   14 years

MY HOME TOWN

I live in TePuke. It is a small place and it has
a lot of shops. I go to town nearly every Friday night
to watch the films at the cinema. I buy my clothes for
school and my jeans in the shops. I go home for the
holidays and I hope to work near TePuke this Christmas.
It is in the Bay of Plenty in the North Island. Other
towns there are Tauranga, and Mount Maunganui. I live
in a village only two miles from TePuke called Manoeka.

There are cow cockeys up our road and a lot of wooden
and brick houses. I go there often for hangis but little
Reg had his first birthday there in May. About 100 people
came and we all gave $15 towards the food.

Daniel TE MONI   14 years

****

VISIT FROM ST STEPHEN'S COLLEGE BOYS

Some boys came to Campbell Park after a visit to
Twizel. The boys from Room 3 showed them around and then
they went to the hall to put on a concert. They wore
yellow shirts and grey trousers. George HERBERT came
over to watch them do their items and then he and some
of the Campbell Park boys got up on the stage and sang
to them. Later the boys had afternoon tea before they
went back to their bus.

Patrick KORA   14 years

that puts all the weight on to the steel to make it go
round". Then we went in the other room where there
was a man putting two steel pieces together and the boys
wanted a go at putting the steel together.

Mainly men work at Humes and it is probably cold
during winter time. The boys go there for work experience.

Walter HUKA   15 years

AUCKLAND

My city is Auckland. I go to all the shops there.
We have a big Easter Show at the show ground. There is
a museum with Maori canoes and caveman's tools. I have
been to Mangere Airport. You watch colour television
while you wait for your plane. The 246 shop is where you buy
clothes. It is a great shop in Queen Street, another big
shop is the Farmers.

On the top storey is a playground for children. We
have the biggest buildings in New Zealand.

The Zoo is big, there are panthers, striped tigers,
and elephants. At Abbot's Way I go riding horses. I
know Auckland very well and I have been all round the
whole city. I know where to go. I always walk and I
never get lost.

George MCGREGOR   13 years

MY HOME TOWN

Nelson is my home town. I like to live on the farm.
I like living in Nelson because it has warm weather and
the water is cool to swim in. There are good shops and
there is a little zoo at the beach. I especially like
the monkeys and the talking parrot. In Nelson there is
the Cathedral Square where children play on the big concrete steps. Not far from there, there is a picture theatre
There is an Airport but no railway station. There is a
big pet shop in Nelson and I like going in to see the
animals for sale. I have bought birds there.

Darryl SMITH 12 years

1977

CAMPBELL PARK SCHOOL
MAGAZINE

INTRODUCTION

A magazine such as this is able to give only
a brief glimpse of various aspects of life at Campbell
Park School. What it cannot convey is the warmth of
relationship which exists between staff and boys in a
very caring sort of way. It cannot easily convey the
feelings which the boys have in terms of pride in their
environment or even a growing pride in themselves.

What I hope it can convey is a feeling that we do
not operate in isolation from the life of the community.
Indeed we derive many benefits from a great number of
caring people and organisations in the North Otago area.
I also hope that these pages convey some idea of the
value of stimulating experiences in terms of the
development of language skills. You may be well assured
that if written language has shown a marked improvement
then spoken language will have improved to an even
greater extent. The social competence of our boys is
aided by easier communication.

F G Aspden
PRINCIPAL

EARLY SETTLERS REMEMBERED

The three cottages occupied by the boys at Campbell
Park are named after early settlers on the school
property.

The junior boys live in TAYLOR HOUSE, the intermediate
boys in DANSEY HOUSE and the senior boys in CAMPBELL HOUSE.

James Parkin TAYLOR settled at Otekaike about 1856.
He sold out to Mr Dansey in 1857. Mr Taylor then shifted
to Southland where he was elected a member of the House
of Representatives in 1859. Eventually he became
Superintendent of the Province of Southland.

William Heywood DANSEY owned the property now used by the
school from 1857 to 1864. Dansey was born in England in
1830 and he came to New Zealand in 1854. A sketch of his
cottage which is on the school grounds is shown on Page 5.
Dansey later built a two storey wooden house which was
demolished before the one on the front cover was built.

Robert CAMPBELL was also born in England. He arrived in
Otago in 1859. Robert Campbell built the big house shown
on the front cover in 1876. He obtained the stone from
the cliffs nearby. The Government bought the school
property from Campbell's nephew Robin Campbell in 1908.
It has been a school since then.

School Log ......

February

15	Miss McCone's class day trip to Bushey.
22	School swimming sports at Kurow.
28	Room 5 outdoor education trip to Huxley Forks begins.

March

2	Dip. Educational Psychology students end two day visit.
3	Inter-school swimming sports at Kurow.
6	Timaru-North Otago Foster Parents' Assn. barbecue on school grounds.
7	Mr John Harris, Melbourne, former librarian at Otago University and nephew of Robert Campbell visited the school.
7	Senior boys from Vocational Class begin a five day outdoor education trip to Kisho.
13	Visit by Inner Wheel.
16	Waitaki Rotary hold meeting at Campbell Park which our senior boys attend.
18	A group of 8 Applied Psychology students visit.
19	Mr L Clyne who had nearly completed 30 years as Engineer passed away.
21	Room 1 with Mr O'Connor begin an educational trip to Queenstown.
23	Mr Doug Moore, South Island soccer coach visited. Mr A.Q. Bruce, Senior Education Officer, Head Office visited.
28	Visit by Windsor C.W.I.
30	Inter-school softball tournament held at Campbell Park.

April

5	Waitaki Lions entertain boys and staff at a barbecue at Awamoko.
19	Timaru Rock Band entertain in hall.
20	Oamaru Round Table visit for games evening.
21	Rev. Marcus Willetts spoke to Anglican group.
22	Campbell House end of term function.
24	Ramsay House visit All Day Bay.
27	Oamaru Motorani Club visit.
27	Room 3 with Mrs Rylance begin a two day trip to Mt Cook.
27	Policy Committee meet at Campbell Park.
29	Senior section athletic sports against Kurow held at Campbell Park.
30	Ramsey House end of term function.

The Principal, Staff and Boys
share with the families of
the late Lou CLYNE, Bruce LLOYD,
William, Timothy and Robin JOHNSON
the sad losses they have suffered
during the year.

STAFF

Principal
F G Aspden

Assistant Principal
F F Walsh

Senior Housemasters
R K Mansfield
B L Walsh

Senior Clerk
Mrs D Bright

Clerks
Mrs N Francis
R S Malthus

Clerical Assistant
Mrs J D Hogan

Typist
Ms A D Gray

Housemasters
T J Mathers
C N Horan
P A Henderson
F Te D Miroti
P P Parsons
R Crosbie
S J Ellwood

Asst. Housemasters
C Albers
R G Chave
R M Lee
J F Forrester
K C Johnstone
R W Worling

Matron
Mrs I F Willis

Sub Matron
Mrs N C Andrews

Cottage Matrons
Mrs K H Irvine
Miss N Savage
Mrs N M Worling

Cottage Sub Matrons
Mrs D N Adams
Mrs G G Campbell
Mrs C M Hughes

Storeman
J Van Der Loon

Driver
Miss D M McAuley

Senior Teacher
R B Willis

Teaching Staff
Miss J R Gibson (Sec)
L B Munro (Sec)
N F O'Connor
Miss K McDona
Mrs B Rylance (Klg)
Mrs D Johnson (Klg)
Miss A Gow (Klg)
G R Gilchrist (Manual)

Teacher Aids
Mrs A Mansfield
Mrs P A M Albers

Matron's Assistants
Mrs W Carter
Miss D Foster
Mrs R McCullough
Mrs J McKenzie
Mrs C Middlemass
Mrs V Willson

Cooks
S G Edens (Senior)
Mrs J Baird
Mrs W Van Der Loon

Seamstress
Mrs M M Curtis

Laundresses
Mrs E M Sullivan
Mrs E Linwood

Instructors
A J R Curtis (Carpenter)
D M R Harris (Carpenter)
L V Linwood (Gardener)
K M Foy (Gardener)
R T Thompson (Engineer)
G R Sutton (Painter)
A R Boyle (Bootmaker)
M G Juckes (Grounds)
J B Taylor (Mechanic)
I J Butler (Poultry)

Engine Drivers
G F Russell
L I McCullough
G W Voigt

Night Attendants
G A Morgan
J A R Johansen
W G Russell
R F Mollen

May

1 Taylor House end of term function.
2 Miss McCone attends week long course at
   Kohitere for teachers.
   Ardgowan W D F F visit.
6 Mr B.J. Waddell resigns to take up teaching
   position in Dunedin.
19 Two day in-service course for staff.

June

1 Buildings Committee meets at Campbell Park.
12 Twelve boys to Oamaru to visit Rotary families.
14 School soccer tournament at Kurow.
16 Miss McDowell and group of student nurses
   visit.
22 Group of boys visit St Lukes, Oamaru to play
   indoor bowls.
24 Anglican boys to St Mary's, Oamaru for tea.
26 Catholic boys to Basilica, Oamaru.
27 Mr F Dunn commenced duty as relieving teacher.

July

7 Senior boys play Kurow at Rugby. St Kevins
   College visit for indoor basketball.
11 Group of special course teachers from Christchurch with Mr Colin Cravish visit for few days.
16 Oamaru Baptist group visit. Concert and games.
17 Visit by Rotary members to see running of
   the annual interhouse relay.
23 Presbyterian boys visit Union Parish, Oamaru.
24 Catholic boys visit Oamaru Catholic families
   for the day.
25 16 boys played annual indoor bowls match against
   Waitaki Power Board and retained the trophy.
29 Mr Aspden spoke at Dunedin Principals' Assn.
31 Anglican boys visit St Lukes, Oamaru.

August

3 Taylor House end of term function.
7 Brother McGrath and Mr W. Clark, Marylands visit.
7 Taylor House visit to Ardgowan C.W.I.
   Seven Catholic boys confirmed by Bishop Kavanagh
   at the Basilica, Oamaru.
10 School choir takes part in Schools' Music
   Festival in Oamaru.
11 Senior rugby versus Kurow at Campbell Park.
12 Boys take part in 10 a-side rugby tournament
   at Kurow.
14 Visit and concert by Te Waipounamu Girls' College.

September

1	Two day in-service course for staff.
6	Visit by Mr John doest, former Assistant Principal and now Senior Institutions Officer with the Department of Social Welfare.
7	Mr L.W. Gandar, Minister of Education visited the school.
10	Parks and Reserves administrators hold meeting at Campbell Park and are shown around by boys.
11	Oamaru United A.F.C. play boys and staff. Visitors won 2 - 0.
19	15 boys play indoor bowls at Otekaieke.
25	48 boys visit Rotary families in Oamaru.
27	Policy Committee meet at Campbell Park.
28	Cross Country at Otematata.
30	School Maori Culture group performs at Oamaru Library.

October

6	Mrs Tawhiwhirangi, Senior Community Officer, Department of Maori Affairs visited the school.
8	Boys take part in Anti-Litter Day.
16	Presbyterian boys to Kurow - church then visit with families.
22	Dansey House hold Labour Weekend camp at Maeraki.
29	Oamaru Youth Orchestra performs at school.

November

14	Mr H. D. Ray, Regional Superintendent of Education visited school.
2	Visit by Waihao Forks C.W.I.
20	Visit by Oamaru Rotary Club for cricket, swimming and barbecue.
26	Salvation Army band visit. Sports and concert.

December

1	Religious Instruction break-up.
5	School winning house outing.
9	Campbell House end of term social.
10	Dansey House end of term function.
12	Taylor House end of term function.

Dansey's Cottage (1880s)

Staff

Front row: Miss Gibson, Mr B Walsh, Mrs Bright, Mrs Andrews, Mrs Willis, Mr P Walsh, Mr Willis, Mr Aspden, Mrs Hughes, Mrs Worling, Mrs Francis, Mrs Sullivan, Mrs Irvine, Mrs Adams, Mr Mansfield.

Second row: Miss Foster, Mrs McCullough, Mrs Middlemass, Mrs Willson, Mrs McKenzie, Miss Gow, Miss McCone, Mrs Campbell, Miss McKay, Ms Gray, Mrs Hogan, Mrs Carter, Mrs Linwood, Mrs Baird, Mrs Curtis, Miss Savage.

Third row: Mr Worling, Mr Parsons, Mrs Rylance, Mrs Johnson, Mr Chave, Mr Van Der Loon, Mr Hiroti, Mr Henderson, Mr Crosbie, Mr Albers, Mr Foy, Mr Horan, Mr Gilchrist.

Fourth row: Mr Malthus, Mr Linwood, Mr Curtis, Mr G Russell, Mr Adams, Mr Earle, Mr Johnson, Mr Harris, Mr McCabe, Mr O'Connor, Mr Juckes, Mr Thompson, Mr Taylor, Mr Voigt, Mr Lee.

Back row: Mr Forrester, Mr Goodwin, Mr Mathers, Mr Lloyd, Mr Ellwood, Mr Dunn.

Absent: Mr McCullough, Miss McAuley, Mrs Mansfield, Mrs Albers, Mr W Russell, Mr Morgan, Mr Johansen, Mr Wollen, Mr K Johnstone, Mr Butler.

Gymnasium

Opposite: Looking down on the school grounds and towards the staff village. The foundations of Campbell's homestead were laid in 1876. The senior boys cottage, Campbell House, is right centre; classrooms and Administration Centre in foreground.

CAMPBELL HOUSE

Front row: Kevin Keetoh, Gary McGlenaghen, Keith Lanceley, Douglas Beck, Robert Jefferies, Craig Pritchard, Arnold Kutia, Charles Harden, Ricky Jonathan, Phillip Tanginetua, Thomas Keranga, Brian Sadler.

Middle row: David McLintock, Richard Matika, Mark Haddon, Michael Antonievic, Philip Butler, Chris Nahia, Fred Waitai, George Herbert, Keith Naber, Stephen Read, Michael Newton.

Back row: Roger Johnson, Duane Tito, William Phelps, Daniel Te Moni, Michael Bruce, Phillip Simon, Danny Cotton, Ricky Te Kiha, Suny Kawanga, Joe Tuapawa, Leslie Robb.

DANSEY HOUSE

Front row: Darryl Crossie, Lance Tasharu, Peter Marli, Michael New, George Jefferies, Simon Tutauha, Isaac Hamilton, Harold Loncaster, William Jack, Darryl Smith, James Neil, David Gay, Clarence Beran.

Middle row: Patrick Lloyd, Jason Kiu, Earl Newton, Timothy Tihi, Shaun McCarthy, Kevin Hotter, Bunny Nahi, Ernest Elwara, Robert Johnston, Peter Friday, Patrick Kora, Leslie Poaru.

Back row: Jackie Taitoko, Terence Ormsby, Patrick Harris, Arthur Kelly, Ricky Davis, Kevin Froggatt, Wayne Bramley, Lionel Phillips, Iulio Faauga, Mark Higgins, Brian Harmer.

TAYLOR HOUSE

Front row: Ian George, Stephen Paramore, Paul Strudwicke, Berry Brown, Ricky Allan, Richard Evans, Raymond Robinson, Wayne Callon, Michael Flowers, Barry Ryder.

Middle row: Phillip Baker, Frank Smith, Gary Chambers, Kevin Gray, Bruce Cotter, Ian Strom, John Whitlow, James Napana, Steven Wycliffe, Simon Ridout.

Back row: Sheru Singh, Spencer Kerensia, Andrew Scott, Shane Taitoko, Richard Murtagh, Kevin Hosking, Billy Stubbing, Peter Haskell, Lance Tawa.

Old stone stables

Life at School

Top left: Philip Butler at work in the bootshop where
he has the opportunity to try canvas work, leatherwork
and upholstery.

Top right: A snug corner in Taylor House.

Centre left: Ricky Davis works on his carving in the
manual training shop. Woodwork gives many boys and their
families a sense of pride of achievement.

Centre right: Stman Tanauha is checking his times tables
on a special tables calculator.

Lower left: "The end of a long day and my feet are tired,"
says Kevin Gray.

Lower right: Lionel Phillips has many games available to
him at Campbell Park - tennis, fives, snooker, darts,
soccer, cricket, hockey, softball and indoor bowls are
some of them.

WINTER
Snow is cold
White as white
Sheep walk in the cold snow

The wind blows the snow down from the hilltops
It blows the snow down from the high trees
It blows it on the ground to freeze.

Arnold KUTIA (15 years)

Snow covers the trees
The animals go and hide
In winter we play games
Rugby, soccer, skating
Volleyball, badminton and skiing.

Thunder sounds
Nights are longer
Leaves are off trees
Birds and animals search for food
Winter for them is cold and lonely.

Roger JOHNSON (15 years)

S now, soft, steep,

N ice, new, neat,

O ld, odd, overpowering,

W hite, watery, wet.

Peter HASKELL (12 years)

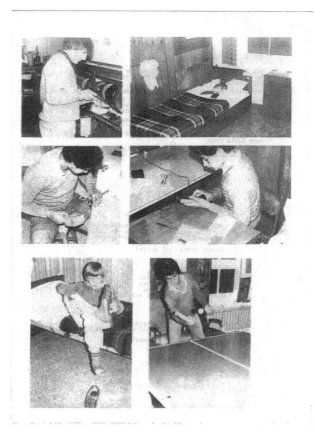

Opposite Top:

Gymnasts - our medal winners.

Front row: Peter Maskell, Douglas Beck, Charles Harden, Billy Stubbing, Lance Tann.

Back row: Timothy Tihi, Tony Kawenga, Michael New, Patrick Harris.

Opposite Middle:

Room 5 Educational Trip to Huxley Forks

Michael New, Lionel Phillips, Sharn Singh, Shane Tsitoko, Frank Smith, Roger Johnson, George Jefferies, Ernest Kiwara, Mr 5 Lloyd.

Opposite Lower:

Safety in numbers - learning the correct way to cross.

Joe Tuapara, Keith Maher, Robert Jefferies, Miss Gow.

Room Five's Trip

On Monday we got ready to go to the camp. We boys went to help Mr Willis so he could get ready. After that we got ready to go but Mr Lloyd went back and got his camping gear. We saw Mr Willis at the garage then he told us to go on. We stopped at Lake Aviemore. Mr Willis was explaining about Lake Aviemore. We went on and stopped at Otematata. Mr Willis was in front. We stopped at the Ahuriri River to have lunch then we had a swim. Mr Willis stopped at Lake Ohau. Mr Willis explained about the lake. We went on. We saw a little river ahead. So Mr Willis had a drink of water. We went up and down the moraines.

When we got to Monument Hut we got our packs and took them to the hut. Mr Lloyd took the boys to put their tent up. We got the food and put it in the hut and I got the fire going - so did Sharn then Mr Lloyd and Mr Willis cooked the food. We had a wash and tea. After that we went to bed. On Tuesday we got our pack and we had our breakfast in the morning about half past seven. We went in the bush and around the other side of the river. We had a practice getting across to the other side of the water. Mr Lloyd and Mr Willis went across and then we had a go. We went on our way. We stopped and had a look at the regrowth trial. Mr Willis explained about it. Then we walked our way down the bush. We stopped at the swing bridge and we went across one by one. We had the dog with us. First was Mr Lloyd and then we came across to the other side. We walked through the bush and came to a little stream then we had our lunch. We saw some snow up in the mountains. We carried on until we came to some rocks. I saw Mr Lloyd and Lionel. I saw the hut from one of the hills we walked across.

We got to the hut about three. After that we got our packs and put the food out. Some boys went up to get wood for the fire. We went up the bush for a walk.

When we came to the hut Mr Lloyd gave us a bunk.
Lionel and Roger went up ahead. They found a swing
bridge down the bush. We had tea and Mr Lloyd read us
a story.

On Wednesday we went for a walk up the north branch
of the Hunley River. We went the other way. We went down
on the rock and then in the bush. Some of us got stuck
in the piri-piri. We got to the other side. We went on.
We stopped and had a rest. Mr Willis said we could find
just one weta for two changing bells but no one had found
one so we went down through the rocks. Some of us had
piri-piri in our socks. We went to find a place to have
our lunch. Some of us had a swim in cold water. Some of
the boys saw the hut from the top of the hill. They said
that it had a yellow roof. Then we had about half an
hours rest before we went back to the hut. Shane had found
a weta. Mr Willis was explaining about mosses and lichens.
We went on walking back to the other hut.

We came back to Campbell Park on the Friday.

Ernest KIWARA (13 years)

Mt Cook

We left Campbell Park School at 10.30 a.m. We stopped
at Twizel. We watched slides about glaciers and rivers.
We played on a scraper, the bulldozer and the grader.
We had lunch at Twizel Park. We saw the Tasman River.
We got to the NZ Alpine Club hut about 3 p.m. We unpacked
the bus.

We went to Mt Cook National Park. We saw some stuffed
birds and animals and the stuffed deer and the flowers.
We saw Mt Cook. Mt Cook is the biggest mountain in New
Zealand. We went to see Lake Pukaki. We saw glaciers with
plenty of ice. We walked up the Hooker Valley and crossed
the Hook River on two swing bridges. Mr Willis took us in
the bus to the Ball Hut where we saw the Tasman Glacier.

We stayed one night and came back in time for tea.

Kevin HOSKINGS (12 years)

PLACES VISITED ON SCHOOL TRIPS

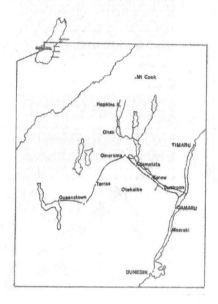

Queenstown Visit

After we had left Campbell Park we had lunch at
Lindis Pass. We stopped at Omarama to swap boys to
Mr O'Connor's car and we looked at the engine of the
mini-bus. We stopped at Tarras for refreshments and
stayed for 10 minutes. On our way to Cromwell we stopped
at the Glassford's place.

We went to Coronet Peak. We went up in the mini-bus.
It was a steep hill going up. We got to the top and it
was a good view. We got our ticket and we got in the
chair lift. We went to the top - it was three miles up.
But I was scared a bit.

We went on the Kon Tiki raft. It took us two hours.
It was a slow river. If they get rain for 24 hours the
river floods. When we went down the river they fed the
seagulls with bread. One boy threw a stone at a seagull.
It was unconscious for two minutes. When we got back we
had a cup of coffee.

On Monday night we went to the pictures. The first
one was about Robot and the second one was about black-
mailing money from a bank and in the end they got killed.

We went to the airport and we had a look at the
helicopter. They were pulling a helicopter to bits.
Every 50 hours they check the parts in the hangar. They
also had a jet helicopter.

Craig PRITCHARD (15 years)

Night Creepers

Last night Isaac, Patrick, Peter, Mr Hiroti and
some of the boys were coming back from the castle.
Michael Bee was coming ahead when Isaac shut the door on
him. Everyone was laughing because he was panicking on
the other side of the door.

After about five minutes everything quietened down
and when Isaac and Patrick and Peter went back in. Patrick
and Peter shut the door on Isaac. Isaac was panicking on
the inside of the door because there was no light on in
the castle. Peter and Patrick crept in there and made
funny noises and that made Isaac really panic and his
voice was echoing through the castle for a while. Patrick
and Peter were creeping around the castle while Isaac
was banging on the door telling Mr Hiroti to open it.
Isaac thought that he might get attacked from behind.
Mr Hiroti was getting annoyed and then he said, "Hang on
damn you!"

Some of the boys were walking around while the rest
were wondering what the excitement was about. Peter and
Patrick Kena went out the other door past the surgery and
barber's room. Isaac saw the door open and he panicked
because he thought that it might be ghosts. He nearly
jumped out of his pants and at that moment Mr Hiroti
opened the door and Isaac ran out so fast that he thought

he was flying. Everything quietened down after that
and then everybody went back to the cottage not
telling anybody what happened. But we told the boys
at school the next morning.

Brian HANNER (14 years)

My Life at Campbell Park

The first time I arrived at Campbell Park I
started off in Taylor House. Since then I have been
behaving myself. I have been through all the cottages.
The cottage I was in before was Denesy House. Everything
has changed. The clothing room has been done up, the rec
room and their outside room done up too.

I am in Campbell House now because of my age. In
Campbell House we work around the place and we only go
to school on Tuesday, Thursday and Friday mornings till
lunch time. Some boys work on the grounds and some in the
laundry. I am working for the storeman. His name is Mr
Van Der Leon. Every week he writes a report on how I
behave. In our cottage we play snooker, pool and table
tennis. On Wednesday night we have a group meeting and Mr
Mansfield comes up and reads all our reports to us and
tells us what group we are in.

Every two weeks six boys go to Work Training. Mr F
Walsh recommends them to go. We have competitions in our
cottage sometimes. Right now we are playing off our table
tennis. At the end of the term we play for the cup. Our
champ last term was Chris Mahia and our pool and snooker
champion was Fred Waitai. At the end of the term we have
a social where girls come out to enjoy themselves and so
for the boys they do the same.

I have been watching the British Lions four games.
On Friday night I have band practice with Mr Geoff Sargent.
In the weekend we clear up in the cottage until 10 o'clock
then we play games until lunch time. Some boys clean out
the gym and some clean out the assembly hall. In the afternoon we play soccer against Comairs. On Saturday night we
play games and watch TV. "A" groupers watch the late movies.

On Sunday we have films at the hall and we have
canteen on Friday mornings and the Housemaster lets us
know how much pocket money we have. Some boys bank their
money and save up.

Sometimes people take us out for weekends. Some
teachers take us out sometimes for tea. Lately I have
been to Miss Gibson's and Miss McCone's for tea.

I only can say about this place that I like it very
much and I am hoping to leave some time in the next year.

Ricky JONATHAN (15 years)

How Maui Captured the Sun

Once upon a time there lived a boy named Maui and
he had brothers who were jealous of him because he had
the magic jawbone of his grandfather. Maui could do
anything with it.

One day Maui made up a plan. He asked his brothers
if they could help him but one of them said, "The sun
will burn us all up," and Maui said, "We shall get some
strong flax and make rope out of it."

Early one morning they watched the sun go by quickly.
The brothers hid all day but when it came to nightfall
again Maui said, "We shall not wait any longer. We must
walk to where the sun rises." So early next morning they
waited until it rose a bit higher than they threw the
rope on to the sun and tangled it while Maui bashed it
with the magic jawbone until the sun gave in.

Maui and his brothers were so happy because they
could have enough play and enough time to work. That's
why the days are so short and so long.

Terence ORMSBY (14 years)

Loneliness

One day I took a walk in the bush, all by myself.
I wasn't very far in the bush so I went deeper and deeper
into the bush. All of a sudden I fell into a big, deep
hole. I could not climb out. What was I going to do?

Two days went past. My mother must have been really
worried. I was hungry and cold. Then I heard people's
voices. I kept trying to scream out "Help! Help! Help!"
Then a man shouted, "Did you hear that screaming? It must
be those pesty possums up in the trees."

Then at least a week had gone past. I was getting
weaker and weaker. I was very lonely and there was nothing
I could do to get out. I kept saying to myself "What am
I going to do?" I was so weak I could not stand on my
feet. I just fell over. I was getting very sick. There
was no water around. Then I heard thunder and it started
to rain and rain. It was pouring down and then it suddenly
stopped. I was very unhappy.

Suddenly I heard voices, so I screamed out "Help!
Help! Help!" I really hoped that they had heard me. Then
a man said, "Look at this deep hole." Then I screamed out,
"Help me, there's someone down here." They turned on the
big torch and they saw me lying on the ground, but I was
not moving so they went down the hole and brought me out.
I was starting to wake up and I kept saying, "Where am I?
Where am I? The man gave me food and drink and put me in a
sleeping bag. Two men picked me up and started to carry me
out of the bush. When we got out there was a police car
waiting and the policeman looked carefully at me and I
heard him say, "That is the boy who was reported missing

My Garden

I have a garden which has nice lovely growing
vegetables in it. I have pumpkins, cabbages, leeks,
beans and potatoes. Vegetables are nice and healthy
and they are also crunchy. You must not waste vegetables because over in the other countries some people
don't even have some of these which we have. So that's
why the teachers at Campbell Park say to us you must
eat all your vegetables which you have got on your
plate.

Now getting back to my garden I have to look
after it and make sure that they get water at night.
You must make sure that your garden is not full up with
weeds because they will just spread and you will have
a hard job cleaning your garden.

Some people have big vegetable gardens because
they might have a lot of vegetables growing for their
families. Some people sell their vegetables to make
money. If vegetables are to be well grown in gardens
they must have the right soil or dirt. The ground must
never be hard because the garden won't have much
moisture in the ground for the vegetables to grow.
You must try and get the ground as soft as you can then
you will find out you will end up with a nice well
looked after garden with nice vegetables.

Some people use big machines if they have got
paddocks of corn or peas growing and they call in these
tractors or trucks and then they get all the corn and
peas and then take them away to factories and put them
in packets and then sell them to people.

Arthur KELLY (14 years)

Softball Tournament

On the 30 March we had 300 children here to play
softball. It was a good day. Jason Kiu's team came
second. Daniel Te Moni led the yellow team and they came
third. The boys from room 5 were the umpires.

The day before, our class made toffee apples in Miss
Gibson's classroom. We sold them in the lunch hour and
the boys and girls enjoyed the toffee apples. We didn't
have any to sell after school.

We had our lunch under the oak tree. The visitors
also had their lunch in their own school groups. During
the lunch hour some of the girls and boys played on our
flying fox.

Gary CHAMBERS (13 years)

```
S  snow
       flow
           low
N  nice
          ice
             dice
O  old
         cold
             bold
W  wet
        met
            set
```

Richard MURTAGH (13 years)

Indoor Basketball Report

On 4th August two Campbell Park teams went to play basketball against St Kevin's and Weston. St Kevin's won 21 - 16. Before we got into Oamaru we spent our canteen money. When we got to St Kevin's they were waiting to start. Then we got on with the games. But after the first half we changed David Gay for Lance Taehara. Then we had to play Weston and we won 15 - 3.

Simon TUTAUHA (14 years)

Rugby

On Friday, 12 August we went to Kurow to play rugby football. The under 6 stone team were on first then the under 5 stone were on at 11.30 a.m. and on again at one o'clock.

We had a good time in Kurow. When we were waiting for our games we had to play around and do nothing for an hour and doing nothing - that was too tiring for me.

Gary CHAMBERS (13 years)

Things I Like

My name is Steven Wycliffe. I come from Auckland. I like being at Campbell Park. It is very good here. I like all the colours in the garden. I like the fire engine.

We learn maths and words in school. In the cottage we learn how to work. My job is to help to clean the rec room. I like going home to see Mum too.

Steven WYCLIFFE (10 years)

My Friend

My name is Michael
Flowers. I have a friend.
His name is Mr O'Connor.
He gave me a ride on his
motor bike. He draws
pictures in my book. He
lets me play with his
typewriter. He is a good
friend.

Michael FLOWERS (12 years)

Myself

My name is Ricky Allen. I come from Rotorua.
I am a Maori. I am nine. I like sports especially
cricket and softball.

I have a shower every night. I have got happy
brown eyes and curly black hair.

I am naughty sometimes because I throw stones.
Mr Willis straps me if I throw stones. I play on
the park and on the bars. I am always busy. After
school today we have shoe change that's all.

Ricky ALLEN (9 years)

Moon Man

My name is Octopus. I come from the moon. I am
300 years old. I am orange all over. I have six legs.
Three legs are fat and three legs are skinny. My eyes
are pink and blue. My hair is green and it looks like
a mop. I live in a space house with my mother and
father and ten brothers and twenty-five sisters. We
play Super family and Batman game together.

We travel in our moonmobile but we can fly as
well. We fell off the moon and that is how we came to
earth. I don't like it here much because I can't fly.

James RAPANA (10 years)

War

We went to the war Ian Strum and me. It was really
scary at night time. The aeroplanes were bombing us.
We died of thirst. The rest of them were still fighting.
A lot of tanks were still firing bullets. We had gone
to our grave.

Wayne GALLOW (12 years)

WINTER SPORT

This winter our
sports fields have
again resounded to the
thud of the leather
balls. This time, more
so than in previous
years, both the oval as
well as the round ball
has been in evidence.
While soccer remains the
game most suited to all
our boys quite a number
of enjoyable Rugby games
have also been played
this year.

SOCCER

As usual our season
started off with our three
cottages entering teams
in the Oamaru competition.
The under 13 and under 15
year olds travelling the
36 miles to Oamaru and back most Saturday mornings while
the senior boys team travelled to Oamaru in the after-
noons. Some Saturdays we had the town teams visit us for
home games and it was a pleasure to be able to entertain
them on our own well maintained grounds. Unfortunately
the cost of travel must be affecting people's pockets as
we didn't have quite as many home games as I believe we
should have had.

Of all three teams competing our 15 year olds gave
the best showing ending up in the upper half of the
competition table. Many of our boys improved with each
game and I'm sure if they continue to improve next season
we could well have a North Otago Representative from our
school

RUGBY

With the influx of new housemasters and teachers we
have a rekindled interest in rugby and it has been good
to see the sports fields having the dual role for a change.
Naturally our boys are keen to play rugby and the chance
to play the national game has great appeal to many of the
boys, particularly the bigger, more robust boys.
During the season two games were played against Kurow Area
School; one at home which we lost and one away which we
won. Both games generated great interest from both boys
and staff and even though we are now well into our summer
sports we still have the question from the boys "When are
we going to have our next rugby game?"

B E Mansfield (Senior Housemaster)

Holiday Under the Sea

We went under the sea for a holiday. We saw a
lot of different fish. Some were friendly. They were
all bright colours.

We saw a whale and an octopus fighting. We saw
a shark get shot with a beam of light to stop it
eating the fish at the fish farm.

One day we put on our skin diving suits and went
out to ride on dolphins. Most of the time we rode in
submarines. We fed a friendly whale every day. We
called him Moby Dick. We would like to go back one day.

Class Story by Room 2.

Spooky Town

Old people live in Spooky Town and they go to other
people's places to scare them. They go out to the
cemetery to pray for people.

There is a spooky castle next to the cemetery and
there is a lady in there with snakes in her hair. She has
got power to make people die. She buries the people who
die in Spooky castle. The people turn to stone.
A vampire came to dig up the graves but the bodies were
all stone. The old lady didn't like the vampire so she
stuck a stick in his heart.

Rowan XXXXX (8 years)

CROSS COUNTRY

When I went to the Cross Country I was not sure
where I was going to come. I was a bit shy. I did not
want to go but I thought I might come somewhere if I tried.

When I started I was with another boy and he was a
good runner. I tried to keep up with him. I did and came
in 6th place. I was going to give up but I had to keep
going so I did and I was pleased with myself.

Lance XXXX (14 years)

RUBBISH

On Saturday October 8 Bunesy and Taylor House boys went
on a rubbish collection from Campbell Park to Kurow. We
found broken bottles in the grass and lots of other rubbish.
PEOPLE SHOULD NOT LITTER. They should care for their town
and country. When people are in their car they should not
throw rubbish out the window. They can take it to the
nearest rubbish bin or keep it till they get home.

Peter FRIDAY (15 years)

Pat Walsh
Assistant Principal

Bruce Willis
Head Teacher

Miss Joan Gibson
Deputy Head Teacher

Owen Payne
Senior Residential
Social Worker

Bernie Walsh
Senior Residential
Social Worker

Chris Albers
Senior Residential
Social Worker

Mrs I Fay Willis
Matron

Steve Juckes
Chief Instructor

Jim Manning
Administration Officer

Top: The classroom block today. Centre: Campbell Park School today covers an area of approximately 100 acres and has a staff village of 36 houses and flats.

Below: The school staff 1977.

Left: Cottage C, now Taylo
House, erected in 1915 fro
locally milled pine. "I do
not think any of these buil
dings - there are three wh
might be described as hands
some villas, costing over
2000 pounds each - will re
anything like a permanent
structure" Hon J.T. Paul M
(Oamaru Mail, 9.3.1918)

Right: It would be difficult
to estimate the tonnes of
rocks transported by boys
building rockeries in the
1920s.

Left: With a roll as hig
200 in 1938, dormitory s
was strictly limited. "A
moment, before the build
are occupied, the study
warped to such an extent
the plaster is falling i
several rooms and there
ominous cracks in others
Hon J.T. Paul, MLC.

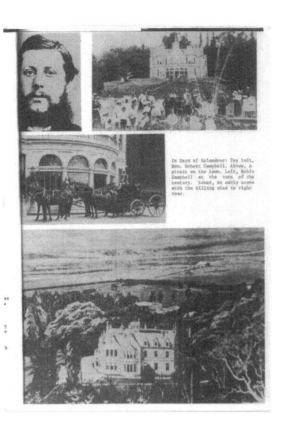

In Days of Splendour: Top left, Hon. Robert Campbell. Above, a picnic on the lawn. Left, Robin Campbell at the turn of the century. Lower, an early scene with the killing shed to right rear.

**MEETING WITH CONFIDENTIAL LISTENING & ASSISTENCE SERVICE
LETTER**

Confidential Listening and Assistance Service
Ratonga Matatapu mō te Rongo me te Āwhina

2 July 2010

Mr Darryl Smith
Alpine View Holiday Park
650 Main South Road
Templeton
CHRISTCHURCH 8042

Dear Darryl

MEETING WITH CONFIDENTIAL LISTENING AND ASSISTANCE SERVICE

Thank you for expressing interest in attending a Panel Meeting to speak about your concerns in State care prior to 1992.

Your meeting time with the panel members of the Confidential Listening and Assistance Service has been scheduled is as follows:

Date: **Thursday 27 July 2018**
Time: **9am**
Venue: **Latimer Hotel, 30 Latimer Square, Christchurch**

What to expect
I plan to meet you when you arrive at the venue – however if I am busy with the previous participant please let the reception staff know that you are here for the **Panel Meeting** and they will direct you to a waiting area. I will be with you as soon as possible. Please note that there is **no need to arrive any earlier than 9am** or you may have to wait unnecessarily.

When we meet I will show you to a private waiting room where there will be refreshments available. Once you are ready you will be escorted to the Panel meeting room. You will have up to an hour and a half to speak with the Panel. After the meeting I will meet with you again. You will need to allow two hours in total of time from 9am.

Who to bring
You are welcome to bring two people with you to support you while you speak with the Panel. Generally support people do not have speaking rights, but if you would like your support person to say anything for you, please tell the Panel when you arrive.

Meeting with the Panel
If you wish, the Panel Chair will offer the opportunity for a ritual to open the meeting. This may be a prayer, a karakia, a poem or a reading. Of course you can choose to just start the meeting without an opening. The Chair will welcome you and introduce the Panel members (3 in total) and then ask you to introduce yourself and to introduce any support people you bring.

PO Box 2905, Lambton Quay, Wellington 6145 •
Email: info@listening.govt.nz • Phone 0800 336 987
Administered by The Department of Internal Affairs Te Tari Taiwhenua

It will then be your opportunity to talk about your concerns and your experiences. The Panel may ask questions to check they understand or to clarify something. Sometimes the Panel may suggest a short break during the meeting and you can also ask for a break if you wish to.

What you tell the Panel will be confidential (unless you tell the Panel that you are very worried about hurting yourself or someone else). Any information you give will not be made public.

Tikanga Maori
If you would like a Kaumatua or Kuia on the panel or supporting you please let me know. If you wish to speak to the Panel in Te Reo please let me know and I can arrange an interpreter. Likewise, if you wish to speak in another language, please let me know.

Preparing for the Meeting
If you would like some help to work out how you would best like to present your concerns to the Panel, and to prepare for the meeting I will be happy to assist you.

Transport
Please discuss any transport difficulties with me so that your needs can be addressed. In some instances it may be possible to refund travel costs to attend the meeting.

Recording the Meeting
If you wish your meeting to be recorded please let the Panel know on the day of the meeting. The recording will be treated as confidential and you will be given a copy on CD. The service will keep a copy of the recording on a secure database but this will be destroyed at a future date.

Documents/Records
You are welcome to bring any documents or records with you that will help you give your account.

After the Meeting
After the meeting you are welcome to go return to the private waiting room for some light refreshments until you feel ready to leave. I will be available during this time to talk with you about any follow up assistance that has been agreed by the Panel.

If you need any special assistance for the meeting or have any questions, please telephone me 0800 356 567.

Yours sincerely

Shelley Gabrielle
FACILITATOR

ARTICLE IN THE OTAGO DAILY TIMES ABOUT DEMANDING A ROYAL COMMISSION

Abuse victims demand Royal Commission